Praise for
Beautiful Smoothie Bowls

"What a refreshing look at smoothies! Healthy smoothies are essentially nutrient-dense foods through a straw, and yet one of the joys of eating is seeing the ingredients of our food and chewing them. Bravo to Carissa Bonham for giving us both in her rainbow-colored goodness-packed recipes. These beautiful bowls are part-smoothie goodness, part sprinkles of fruit, nuts, seeds, and other wholesome delights. You cannot help but fall in love with them. A beautifully done book which leaves you feeling satiated and guilt-free!"

—Farnoosh Brock, author of *The Healthy Smoothie Bible* and *The Healthy Juicer's Bible*

"Carissa is Queen of Smoothie bowls. I love her recipes and recommend this book for anyone who wants to start or maintain a healthy lifestyle."

—Leah Segedie, founder of Mamavation and ShiftCon

"I've always been a fan of smoothies, but I have to say that they never really filled me up and left me satisfied. That is, until smoothie bowls came on the scene! Carissa and her team have put together a beautiful book featuring beautiful food. Not only do you have eighty recipes to choose from, but you also get a full education about why smoothie bowls are superior, what ingredients to use, and how to maximize your bowl's nutrition. Even those on special diets will be able to enjoy the flavorful creations Carissa presents in this stunning book!"

—Jessica Espinoza, wellness coach and founder of DeliciousObsessions.com

"One of the issues I have with eating healthy is that I get bored. Bored with the same old same old—all the time. After going through the smoothie bowl recipes in this book, I am inspired! I am excited to try SO MANY of these gorgeous recipes and thanks to this book I don't think I'll ever be bored with 'healthy sweets' again!"

—Amanda Formaro of Amanda's Creative Life, Inc

Beautiful SMOOTHIE BOWLS

80 DELICIOUS AND COLORFUL SUPERFOOD RECIPES TO NOURISH AND SATISFY

CARISSA BONHAM

Skyhorse Publishing

Skyhorse Publishing books may be purchased in bulk at special discounts for sales promotion, corporate gifts, fund-raising, or educational purposes. Special editions can also be created to specifications. For details, contact the Special Sales Department, Skyhorse Publishing, 307 West 36th Street, 11th Floor, New York, NY 10018 or info@skyhorsepublishing.com.

Skyhorse® and Skyhorse Publishing® are registered trademarks of Skyhorse Publishing, Inc.®, a Delaware corporation.

Visit our website at www.skyhorsepublishing.com.

10 9 8 7 6 5 4 3 2 1

Hardcover Library of Congress Cataloging-in-Publication Data

Names: Bonham, Carissa, author.
Title: Beautiful smoothie bowls : 80 delicious and colorful superfood recipes to nourish and satisfy / Carissa Bonham.
Description: New York, NY : Skyhorse Publishing, [2017] | Includes index.
Identifiers: LCCN 2016055655 (print) | LCCN 2017002731 (ebook) | ISBN 9781510719491 (hardcover) | ISBN 97815107195097 (Ebook) | ISBN 9781510719507
Subjects: LCSH: Smoothies (Beverages) | Smoothies (Beverages)--Health aspects. | LCGFT: Cookbooks.
Classification: LCC TX840.B5 B43 2017 (print) | LCC TX840.B5 (ebook) | DDC 641.87/5--dc23
LC record available at https://lccn.loc.gov/2016055655

Cover design by Jenny Zemanek
Cover photograph by Carissa Bonham

Paperback ISBN: 978-1-5107-7098-0
Hardcover ISBN: 978-1-5107-1949-1
Ebook ISBN: 978-1-5107-1950-7

Printed in China

For Asher and Kaypha:
May you always know and love what real food tastes like.

Contents

Introduction

This book has been a true labor of love. For more than four years now, I've dedicated my website, Creative Green Living, to helping moms and dads make healthier lifestyle choices that are both beautiful and delicious. British food icon Jamie Oliver once called the idea that healthy food is boring or tasteless "rubbish," and I couldn't agree more. After looking through and sampling some the recipes in this book, I hope you'll agree. Each of these recipes is designed to be both nourishing and delicious—and nice to look at, too!

Although healthy food that tastes delicious has been a personal passion of mine for years, I wanted to make sure this book would bring you more perspectives and taste palates than my own. As such, I partnered with some of the best healthy food bloggers and Instagrammers worldwide when assembling this book. Photos and recipes for their beautiful smoothie bowls appear throughout these pages. If a recipe is not my own, it's clearly marked with the name of its creator at the top of the page with more information about her below the recipe itself. I don't claim to have a monopoly on beautiful, healthy food, and I encourage you to follow these women on their sites and Instagrams so that you can be inspired by healthy food daily. And while you're at it, be sure to follow me on Instagram as both @CreativeGreenLiving and @CreativeGreenKitchen.

I want to personally thank each of these amazing women for contributing to this project. Instead of listing them here, I encourage you to flip to page 211 to check out the recipe contributor credits and see the full list of contributors and read more about them!

May your bellies be full and your bodies be nourished by these recipes. If you have a favorite, let me know on social media (@CreativeCarissa on Twitter, @CreativeGreenLiving or @CreativeGreenKitchen on Instagram). Even better, snap a photo and post it to Instagram with #BeautifulSmoothieBowls and be sure to tag @CreativeGreenKitchen.

How to Use This Book

'm a firm believer that anyone who can both safely use a knife and operate a blender can make a beautiful smoothie bowl. If you're a beginner, be sure to read the chapters before the actual recipes for your crash course in Smoothie Bowls 101—you'll be a smoothie bowl pro in no time!

Every recipe in this book is gluten friendly so if you have celiac or a gluten sensitivity, you're in luck! Now, the "gluten friendliness" of the recipes only goes as far as the ingredients you choose. This means that for recipes that include oats, granola, cereal, or any other prepackaged item, you will want to be sure to read the labels and choose gluten-free options and foods that were not processed in facilities that also process wheat if you have a true gluten allergy or intolerance. If you aren't sensitive to gluten, of course, you can choose any variety of these products that you wish—although I recommend choosing organic whenever possible. This is in large part because some nonorganic farmers use glyphosate (a.k.a. Round Up), an herbicide, in the preparation of their oats and other grains for harvest. Side of Round Up with your smoothie? No thanks! Glyphosate is not permitted in organic agriculture, so that's just one more reason I choose organic as much as possible.

To help you easily find recipes that match your personal dietary preferences, I have labeled each recipe with the applicable labels here:

- Ⓥ **Vegan:** Recipe contains no animal-derived ingredients. You will find fifty recipes with this label, although the remaining thirty are easily adapted to a vegan lifestyle by substituting coconut yogurt for dairy yogurt, plant milk for dairy milk, and agave syrup for honey. One recipe contains gelatin, but it's just as delicious when you leave that ingredient out (or try it with ground chia or flaxseed instead!). All the recipes except the one containing gelatin are vegetarian.

- **(P) Paleo:** Recipe that meets the requirements for most people living a paleo lifestyle. These recipes will not contain any grains, dairy, or highly processed foods, but may contain maple syrup or honey. Recipes containing agave are not labeled as paleo, but in most instances, honey or maple syrup make an excellent paleo substitute. Of the forty-one recipes labeled as paleo, thirty-seven also meet the requirements for Whole 30—what many people would describe as an "extreme version of paleo." For more information on Whole 30, see www.whole30.com.

- **(gf) Gluten Free:** Recipe as-written does not use gluten-containing ingredients. If you are gluten sensitive, you are still responsible for selecting appropriate gluten-free ingredients for prepackaged goods like granola, oats, and cereals that may contain gluten or have been cross-contaminated during the packaging process.

- **(df) Dairy Free:** While the vegan recipes also happen to be dairy free, I wanted to label the sixty-two dairy-free recipes separately because not everyone avoiding dairy due to a milk allergy or lactose intolerance are vegans and also avoiding other animal-derived ingredients like honey. The dairy-containing smoothies usually contain yogurt or dairy milk. In these instances, coconut yogurt or a plant-based milk would be an easy swap to make a smoothie fit a dairy-free lifestyle.

Smoothie Bowl Magic

Taking a pile of fruits and veggies along with a few other ingredients and transforming them into a beautiful and delicious smoothie bowl is like magic to me. Even more magical is the transformation of frozen bananas (or other frozen fruit) into "nice cream"—a low fat, plant based miracle that resembles ice cream in taste and texture with none of the guilt.

Anyone can dump a smoothie into a bowl. The real fairy dust that elevates a smoothie poured into a bowl to the status of "smoothie bowl" is the toppings. Fancy or simple, sprinkled or arranged, smoothie bowls' toppings make or break them. It's easy to make a beautiful bowl that is still relatively simple to put together—which also makes them perfect for impressing brunch guests or even just your Instagram followers.

Why Smoothie Bowls?

The roots of smoothie bowls can be traced back to Brazilian Açaí Bowls. A bowl of mashed açaí berries and other toppings (including savory ones like shrimp and fish!) was a traditional Amazonian dish that started making its way to large Brazilian cities in the 1970s. Eventually frozen açaí pulp was brought to the United States in the early 2000s, and frozen açaí bowls could be found in both California and Hawaii where surfers and sun worshippers would eat them as a healthy meal or snack. Unlike the savory bowls from the Amazon, these were usually blended with bananas and a sweetener of some sort and topped with fruit and granola.

More recently, the idea of an açaí bowl has expanded to include frozen smoothies of all colors both with and without actual açaí. As açaí is no longer a requisite ingredient, the name of the broader phenomenon of frozen smoothies in bowls with toppings is now called a "smoothie bowl" or sometimes a "(name of key ingredient) bowl"—like "pitaya bowl" or "mango bowl." Very thick smoothie bowls with the consistency of soft serve or ice cream are called "nice cream."

Drinkable Smoothies vs. Smoothie Bowls

But what's with the bowl? I would bet you've enjoyed drinkable smoothies through straws at some point. Curious why they're suddenly showing up in bowls instead? Here are the top three reasons I think the smoothie bowl phenomenon has caught on:

They Are Beautiful

More aesthetically pleasing than a smoothie in a cup, smoothie bowls are a way someone can bring fun and creativity to their meals. It's easy to slice a banana and lay it out in a crescent shape on top of a smoothie bowl. Suddenly basic breakfast has turned into a gourmet experience (and one much more Instagram-worthy!). Even if my smoothie bowl doesn't end up on Instagram, I feel like I'm taking better care of myself when I eat a beautiful breakfast.

They Help You Feel Full Sooner

One phenomenon smoothie drinkers often experience is what I call "but I'm still hungry" syndrome. When you drink your calories, it's harder for your brain to realize "I'm full." The result is often that you might drink a 400-calorie smoothie meant to be your meal, but you're still hungry so you go down the street to pick up a sandwich, too. You have now effectively doubled the number of calories you have consumed during lunch time because, according to your brain, you didn't "eat" anything until you got your sandwich. By slowing down and actually *eating* your smoothie with a spoon, your brain gets the time and signals it needs to register a full feeling so you finish your bowl feeling full and fueled up instead of hungry for something else.

The Satisfaction of Chewing

This is related to helping your brain feel full but deserves its own line and I'll tell you why: several years ago, in an effort to lose weight, I joined a program where I had a smoothie for breakfast, a snack, a smoothie for lunch, another snack, and a normal, healthy dinner. In the online support group I was in during my participation, most of the other women noted that they didn't feel hungry on this plan but they *missed eating things*—that is, they missed the feel of eating and chewing. There is a certain satisfaction one can really only get from chewing, and smoothie bowls let you combine the nutritional power of your smoothie with the satisfaction of chewing to create a superior breakfast that is satisfying, nourishing, and packed with the stuff your body needs to stay healthy and power through your day.

Benefits of Blending

Whether you serve it in a glass or a bowl, smoothies are a great healthy choice for lots of reasons. My favorite is that you can cram a whole lot of nutrition into one easy-to-eat bowl with a little help from your blender. While I *could* sit down to eat a small spinach and kale salad, two kiwis, two cups of mixed fruit, a handful of chia and flaxseeds, some nuts, and a glass of coconut water for breakfast—that's a lot of food *and* a lot of chewing! Instead, I can transform these same ingredients into a Pentatonic Kale smoothie (on page 162) and get a great nutritional head start to my day without having to take the time to chew all that food.

Smoothie bowls don't just make a great breakfast! Twelve of the bowls in this book are a thick, scoopable "nice cream" that make the perfect substitute for your previous dessert choices. Instead of curling up on the couch with a pint of Ben and Jerry's after work, try curling up with Purple Dragon Nice Cream (page 206) instead. While the 1,400 calories and 60 grams of fat in a pint of Cherry Garcia could have left you feeling guilty, a big bowl of Purple Dragon has only 413 calories, has 4 grams of fat, and is guilt free—not to mention, you'll also get 226 percent of your recommended daily intake of vitamin C and 66 percent of your daily recommended fiber! Sorry, Ben.

Smoothie Bowl Basics

Remember when I said the only skill sets you need to make great smoothie bowls are the ability to use a knife and operate a blender? I meant it! If you don't have a high-powered blender, you might need to add the ability to use a food processor if you want to make nice cream. Truthfully, parents: with a little safety pep talk from you, your kids could probably make any of the smoothie bowls in this book on their own. If a fourth-grader can do it, I know you can, too!

Equipment

To get your kitchen ready to make a great smoothie bowl, you'll need a few things. You'll be happy to hear that you probably already own most of them! If not, a quick trip to a department store will get you squared away

Blender

The first thing you'll need to whip up an amazing smoothie bowl is a blender. I highly recommend choosing a blender that has a glass jar. While plastic blender jars are lightweight, I have concerns about the chemicals used in the plastics. Even plastic blender jars labeled "BPA free" could still contain BPS or other harmful endocrine disrupting chemicals (that's a fancy way to say "chemicals that mess with your hormones"), and I avoid them for that reason.

I have two different blenders with glass jars at home. The first is a Black & Decker FusionBlade blender. It has flat, non-sharp blades (this makes it easy to clean!) and a glass jar. As a bonus, it came with a small, plastic personal blending jar and a separate blade mechanism to go with it. While I don't use the plastic jar, the blade designed to fit on the personal jar is the perfect size to use with standard mouth mason or canning jars—which is how I use it to make drinkable smoothies on the go. Another feature I like about this blender is that it has three speeds, pulse, and an automatic "smoothie program"—which works like a dream! If you are looking for a high-quality, glass-jarred blender under $100, this is the one I recommend.

If you have a little more money to spend, the second blender I have is a Tribest Dynablend Clean Blender. As of the writing of this book, this is the highest-powered glass jar blender that you can get in the United States. Unlike the FusionBlade, which has plastic as part of the blade housing that touches your food, the Dynablend Clean has no plastic parts that touch your food at all. That means, in addition to making smoothie bowls, this is also a great blender to use for hot food like soup or puréed sauces. The one downside of the Dynablend is that I was hoping I would be able to use it to make both smoothies and nice cream the way expensive plastic blenders can. While it whips up smoothies like nobody's business, it wasn't quite up to the task of replacing my food processor as primary nice cream maker. Truthfully, most blenders can't make nice cream so don't hold that against it. At the end of the day, it is the highest-powered, glass-jarred blender you can get at its price point and that makes it a worthwhile investment. Mine has earned its spot on my counter.

Food Processor

While your blender is the tool you'll need most of the time, a food processor is the ideal way to make nice cream. Most blenders are designed to blend runny and semi-frozen liquids, making them ideally suited for smoothies. Nice cream, on the other hand, is almost entirely frozen fruit with only a few tablespoons of liquid. This difference in the solid food to liquid ratio between a standard smoothie and nice cream is why you need two different tools.

Even though it might seem like a pain to get a second appliance if you don't already own one, you can buy a food processor that will make beautiful nice cream for less than $30. Want to save even more money? In Portland, I often see food processors being sold on Craigslist for $15 to $20—even ones that are brand new in the box! If you've been nursing a premium ice cream habit, your new food processor will pay for itself in just a few weeks when you switch to making nice cream instead.

Silicone Scraper

Smoothie bowls tend to be thicker than the drinkable variety. This makes it easier for them to support your beautiful toppings. It also makes it more likely that your smoothie will stick to the inside of your blender. Having a silicone scraper on hand will make it easy to get every last bit of your smoothie out of your blender while also avoiding the toxic chemicals often found in plastic.

Sharp Knife

A sharp knife is the cornerstone of any well-stocked kitchen. If you've been muddling along with dull knives, now is the time to invest in either a high-quality knife or, at the very least, a knife sharpener. Using a dull knife not only makes your food prep take longer, but it's also dangerous. If you press down on your knife and it causes your food to roll away from you instead of slicing through it, you could get hurt and end up cutting something you don't mean to—like your hand!

Plastic or Silicone Freezer Bag

Most smoothie bowl recipes use some variety of frozen fruit. While it's easy to find frozen berries, peaches, and pineapples pre-frozen in the store, some fruits you will need to freeze on your own. It's a good idea to prep your kitchen for your new smoothie bowl habit by pre-freezing some bananas, avocados, and watermelon chunks in these bags. For bananas and avocados, peel them and cut into chunks. Put the chunks in the bag and pop it in the freezer. For watermelon, cut it into cubes, pat dry with paper towels, and freeze on a cookie sheet before transferring the chunks to a freezer bag. You can use a plastic zip-top freezer bag or a reusable silicone bag for this purpose.

Gizmo Gadgets

A brief stroll through any store with a kitchen department could leave you thinking your kitchen is seriously lacking. Cherry pitters, strawberry corers, avocado slicers, pineapple spiralizers, mango splitters, the list goes on! The truth is: while some of these gadgets can make certain repetitive tasks easier, you don't need most of them. The one gadget I do use on a regular basis is a serrated peeler because it makes quick work of cutting away the peel of soft-skinned fruits like kiwi and peaches. If you don't already own any of these kitchen gadgets, make a few recipes first and see what you like or want to make a lot of before spending money on a gizmo you might not really use. Can't stay away from the store? Let your food preferences be your guide! If you're mad about pineapple, you will probably use a pineapple spiral cutter more often than a cherry pitter.

Measuring Cups (Optional)

When you first start making smoothie bowls, you may be more comfortable measuring the ingredients out the way we've written the recipes. After you get the hang of it and become a smoothie bowl pro, you may abandon your measuring devices altogether—and that's okay! The truth is that unless I am developing a recipe specifically for other people to recreate, I don't usually measure anything in my kitchen. Once you've measured out 1 cup of raspberries a dozen times, you'll start to know what a cup of raspberries looks like and will just start throwing ingredients in your blender like a master bartender. If you're a newbie, though? There's no shame in measuring!

The Anatomy of a Smoothie Bowl

If you have not yet had the pleasure of eating a smoothie bowl, fear not! They are more simple than you might think. Each smoothie bowl in this book has two parts:

Bottom Layer: Smoothie

The smoothie portion of each recipe should make about a pint of smoothie or nice cream. This is the same amount of smoothie you would expect to get if you ordered a "small" at most popular smoothie and juice bars in the United States. Because the recipes in this book involve chewing, you might find yourself surprised at how full you feel after eating what amounts to a small smoothie with toppings!

Top Layer: Toppings

The toppings for each bowl are different. Sometimes there are so many toppings you can hardly tell what color the smoothie underneath is. Others are scanter. I'm a big fan of variety and the recipes reflect that! Flowers are a popular topping both in the book and on Instagram. If you haven't grown flowers yourself, you might not be aware that many kinds of flowers are both beautiful and edible! If you aren't sure if a flower in your yard or garden is edible, leave it off. Of course, my topping suggestions are just that: suggestions. Each recipe tells you how to make the smoothie bowl as pictured, but let your imagination grow wild. Don't be afraid to think outside the recipe.

Smoothie Bowl Troubleshooting

If you aren't already a blending guru, you might run into some hiccups as you embark on your smoothie bowl journey. If you follow the recipes in this book as-written, I'll be able to steer you clear of these problems. My hope, though, is that, as you grow more confident in your smoothie-making skills, you will begin to experiment with making smoothies on your own. Here are some common smoothie problems and ways to solve them.

Problem	Possible Cause	How to Fix It
Smoothie too runny/Toppings sink to the bottom	Not enough frozen ingredients used	Blend in more frozen fruit or ice cubes
Smoothie too chunky/Blender won't blend	• Not enough liquid • Blender underpowered	• Add more liquid while blender is off, stir with spatula, and replace lid before attempting to reblend. • If adding liquid to your smoothie does not help or you have to add so much liquid that your smoothie becomes very runny, it may be time to purchase a new blender.
Smoothie is an unappetizing shade of brown	Attempting to blend red and green ingredients together	• Overpower the brown with highly pigmented purple fruits like blueberries, blackberries, or black raspberries. • Drink it from an opaque cup with a straw (like a travel mug) if the flavor is good but the color is unappealing.

A Rainbow of Nourishing Superfoods

What exactly is a superfood? While the word *superfood* has no specific legal definition, it's commonly used to describe foods that are especially nutrient-dense and beneficial to your body. As there is no "superfood litmus test," the foods worthy of the title *superfood* will vary from person to person and list to list.

"What about the rainbow?" Have you heard the term *eat a rainbow every day*? In general, this is great nutritional advice telling the recipient to eat foods of all different colors to receive well-balanced nutrition. Even without a fancy nutrition-tracking app, by eating a rainbow of colorful whole foods, you can get a pretty good feel for what a balanced diet looks like. Of course, eating a rainbow doesn't count if the rainbow if derived from artificial colors and dyes. Stick to nourishing, whole foods that are minimally processed (if at all) like the ones below.

Meet the Superfoods

Throughout this book, I'll be focusing on thirty different superfoods. Other ingredients will pop in from time to time, but these will be the backbones of most recipes. Some are familiar favorites but others may be new to you. This is by no means an exhaustive list of superfoods, but each one is here because of its specific nutritional profile and ability to make a tasty and beautiful smoothie bowl.

Açaí

Açaí (pronounced *ah-sai-ee*) berries are small, dark purple-black berries that grow on certain types of palm trees—mostly in Brazil and Indonesia. Açaí berries are high in antioxidants, and Amazonian natives claim they have immune-boosting, healing, and energy-boosting properties.

Açaí does not keep for very long after being picked, which explains why you don't see clusters of these berries in your local supermarket's produce section. To prepare them for market, berries are processed so they can withstand shipping. They're most often juiced and bottled or turned into a pulp and then frozen. You can also buy shelf-stable freeze-dried berries or berry powder.

Açaí has a wine-like, strong flavor so most North Americans prefer it blended with a sweeter fruit or with a sweetener like honey or agave. It imparts a beautiful dark purple color to smoothies it is blended into.

Avocado

You might be familiar with avocados in the context of savory dishes like guacamole, but avocados make a great addition to smoothies, as well! High in monounsaturated fat in the form of oleic acid, a diet which includes avocados has been shown to help lower both total and LDL (sometimes called "bad") cholesterol. It's also been shown to increase HDL (sometimes called "good") cholesterol. Aside from the healthy plant fats, avocado flesh is also high in vitamin E, folate, and potassium (almost twice as much as a banana!).

Avocados are notorious for turning from not-quite-ripe to too-far-gone very quickly, so I recommend watching avocados like a hawk until they hit peak ripeness and then quarter, peel, and freeze them to use later in your smoothie recipes.

Avocados are part of the Clean Fifteen—a list put out every year by the Environmental Working Group that ranks the fifteen least pesticide-contaminated fruits and vegetables. Avocados are consistently one of the least pesticide-contaminated produce items (only 1 percent of samples showed any detectable level of pesticides!). While I would never discourage anyone from buying organic produce, when buying avocados, it's okay to save your money and stick with conventionally grown without sacrificing your health.

Banana

If I could give a prize to a superfood for being the most versatile, I just might choose the banana. Bananas are great for eating out of hand, topping smoothie bowls, and for blending into smoothies themselves. When frozen, bananas can by turned into a magical nice cream that would rival any super-premium ice cream from the store.

When most people think about the nutritional profile of bananas, potassium is usually what comes to mind. While bananas are high in potassium, they are also high in vitamin B-6 (just one banana can give you 20 percent of your RDAI) as well as vitamin C. Bananas contain tryptophan—the protein your body uses to make serotonin, a chemical that promote feelings of well-being and happiness. Is this why sitting down with a big bowl of a banana-based nice cream like Mermaid Magic (on page 153) makes you so happy inside? Maybe!

Bananas are a very popular food choice in my house so I always have a bunch of them on hand. In addition to the fresh bananas, I like to keep my freezer stocked with frozen bananas for smoothies and nice cream. To freeze bananas, simply peel them, break into chunks, place in a freezer bag, and pop into the freezer—it's that easy!

Bananas appear white or cream-colored in smoothies, which makes them blend colorlessly into whatever concoction you're whipping up. They also impart a sweet flavor to whatever you're working on, especially if they were allowed to become very ripe before using.

Smoothie Bowl Tip: Always break bananas into the same number of chunks before freezing to make it easier to measure out "one banana" from your bag of chunks. I like to break bananas into six pieces. When a recipe calls for 1 frozen banana, I just pull 6 chunks out of the bag and add them to the blender.

Beets

Beets are a food people seem to either love or hate—although everyone can agree the color is marvelous! Beets can be used raw, like in Pink Kisses (page 89), or cooked, such as in Berry Heart Beets (page 97). Both ways, beets contain powerful phytonutrients that help fight cancer and boost stamina. Even if you've previously turned up your nose at beets before, give one of these recipes a whirl—you just might find your new favorite way to incorporate these into your diet!

Beets come in a myriad of colors and patterns, including a variety called Chioggia, which is striped like a candy cane when you cut into it. Solid-colored beets range from yellowy-orange to pink to deep purple. Take a look around your local farmers' market and pick up a new variety to experiment with! As with all root vegetables, I highly recommend buying these organic whenever possible because they absorb both nutrients and toxins from the soil directly into the portion of the plant that you eat.

Beets of all colors have a tendency to stain whatever they touch, so be mindful of which cutting boards you use and how much of the raw beet juice you allow to get on your hands. You might also want to consider an apron!

Beets will lend an intense color (orange, pink, or purple depending on the variety) and an earthy flavor to your smoothies. Cooking the beets before using them will sweeten them a bit and take an edge off the earthy tones in their flavor profile.

Blackberries

Where I live in the Pacific Northwest, blackberry bushes grow wild in any drainage ditch, field, or other untended plot of land during summer. Some people say you aren't really an Oregonian or Washingtonian until you've been wild blackberry picking in one of the many places wild berries can be gleaned in parks, alongside roads, and more.

Of course, blackberries are also available in produce aisles and at farmer's markets during the summer and in the freezer case year around. Just one cup of these sweet, juicy berries can get you 50 percent of your RDA of vitamin C. Blackberries are also high in vitamin K and anthocyanins—the flavonoids that give the blackberry both its color and power to combat oxidative stress and cancer.

To get berries with the best flavor, pick them wild or find them at your local farmers' market when they are in season at the end of the summer. You may be able to find fresh blackberries in the grocery store, but I have found that grocery store blackberry varieties were chosen not for their superior flavor, but for their ability to withstand the stress of the shipping process without getting smashed. These are beautiful berries to be sure, but are oftentimes bitter and less juicy than locally grown varieties. Frozen blackberries are a great choice, as well. Store-bought frozen blackberries tend to be sweeter than fresh because they were picked at peak ripeness and frozen immediately before being shipped. Whether fresh or frozen, opt for organic, as the nooks and crannies of the berries make it hard to completely wash off pesticides.

While they might appear black at first glance, when smashed or blended into a smoothie, blackberries impart a purple color and a sweet, tangy flavor. The color is strong enough to "override" a smoothie that accidentally turned brown from a bad color combo. If your smoothie's color is looking a little sad, add some "emergency blackberries" to turn it around!

Blueberries

While they don't grow wild as freely as blackberries, blueberries are another quintessential Northwest fruit that definitely belongs in your smoothie bowl. Just like açaí and blackberries, the anthocyanins that give blueberries their color also fight the destructive effects of free radicals in our bodies. They are high in vitamins C and K as well as manganese. The wide variety of phytonutrients in blueberries have been shown to combat the effects of aging, boost focus and memory retention, and support heart health by lowering both LDL (or "bad") cholesterol and blood pressure.

Get fresh blueberries when you can, but frozen berries work well for all applications—even as a smoothie bowl topping. Due to their thin, edible skins, choose organic whenever possible to avoid persistent pesticides that don't wash off easily in your kitchen sink.

In smoothies, blueberries give off a beautiful, purple color and a fresh, berry flavor that combines well with other flavors or sings in harmony with other varieties of berries.

Carrots

Did you know that carrots come in a beautiful rainbow of colors? Orange are the common grocery store staples, but they can also be red, yellow, purple, and black (purple are my personal favorite!). Renowned for being good for your eyes, carrots are exceptionally high in vitamin A—just one medium-sized carrot gives you more than 200 percent of your RDA! The black and purple carrots are also high in vitamin A but with an added boost of anthocyanins—similar to blueberries and blackberries.

I stuck to orange carrots for the recipes in this book because multicolored carrots are not widely available in all grocery stores. If you have a garden, however, definitely grow the purple haze variety. They have a dark purple skin with an orange core, and they're my favorite for eating raw. If you have access to purple carrots, try adding one to any of the purple smoothie recipes that appear near the end of the book for an added boost of vitamin A!

To prepare carrots for use in smoothies (or any other recipe), just give them a good scrub to remove any dirt and cut off the tops and about a quarter inch of the tip. You may have grown up peeling carrots before use, but this is actually entirely unnecessary. A good scrub is all they need! Like all root vegetables, though, be sure to choose organic carrots when available to reduce your exposure to persistent pesticides.

Carrots have a sweet, fresh taste that blends well with other fruits. It pairs especially well with citrus, apple, and ginger. Most colored carrots still have an orange core, so be aware of that when adding them to smoothies. A red carrot won't turn your smoothie a brilliant red like adding a beet will.

Cherries

Available in a variety of beautiful shades of red and sometimes yellow, cherries are not only delicious, but they're also a cancer-fighting powerhouse. Containing high levels of vitamins A and C as well as potassium and anthocyanins, cherries help your body fight inflammation and keep cancer cells in check. For a bigger antioxidant punch, choose ripe, darker-colored cherries.

Fresh cherries are only available for a short time during the early summer. To extend how long they keep, store them in the fridge and don't wash them until right before you are ready to eat them. Stock up on fresh cherries to store in your freezer (pit them first!) or buy them prefrozen year-round.

Cherries are on the Dirty Dozen list—a list of the twelve most pesticide-contaminated fruits and vegetables—which is put out every year by Environmental Working Group. What does this mean? It means that of all the fruits and vegetables tested, cherries ranked as being the seventh most-likely to be contaminated with pesticides in 2016. For this reason, I recommend choosing organic cherries as much as possible!

To prep fresh cherries, rinse them immediately before use and remove the stems and pits. The stems pop right off, but the pits can be a bit tricky. If you don't already own a cherry pitter, you can also use a straw to do the job. Place the cherry on top of a narrow-necked bottle and push down through the center with a reusable straw (disposable straws are too flimsy for this task) to pop the pit into the bottle. Although a bit tedious, you can also use a paring knife to carefully cut the cherry in half and pop out the pit.

Cherries bring a variety of flavors depending on which type you use in your recipes. Dark, sweet cherries can have a jammy or wine-like flavor while tart cherries are much brighter. Yellow cherry varieties such as Rainier will blend well into most recipes while dark cherries will bring a deep red tone to whatever they are added to.

Not sure when to spend the extra money to buy organic? Here are my suggestions for which common smoothie-bowl ingredients are worth the splurge.

Choose Organic Whenever Possible	Okay to Buy Conventional
Apples, Beets, Blackberries, Blueberries, Carrots, Cherries, Dragon Fruit/Pitaya, Ginger, Granola, Green Tea/Matcha, Honey, Kale, Kombucha, Nuts and Seeds, Oats, Peaches, Pomegranate, Pumpkin, Raspberries, Spinach, Strawberries, Yogurt	Açai, Avocado, Coconut, Honeydew, Kiwi, Mango, Oranges, and other citrus fruit (unless planning to eat the peel), Pineapple, Watermelon

Considerations for these selections include presence of persistent pesticide residue in EPA test, whether item is a common GMO commodity or at risk for GMO contamination, and if non-organic versions undergo processing which exposes them to undesirable chemicals.

Chia

Tiny nutritional powerhouses, just 1 ounce of chia seeds (about 2 tablespoons) contains 30 percent of the RDA for manganese, 30 percent of the RDA for magnesium, and 27 percent of the RDA for phosphorus. That's not all! Chia seeds are also high in protein, calcium, fiber, potassium, antioxidants, zinc, and B vitamins as well as omega-3 fatty acids. Whew!

Chia seeds have the unique feature of absorbing liquid and turning into a gel. You can make a simple "chia pudding" by combining 3 tablespoons of chia seeds with 1 cup of coconut milk and a splash of vanilla extract. Stir together and refrigerate for 4 hours. You will be amazed by what happens! Chia seeds can absorb up to twelve times their weight in liquids and transform from a liquidy mess into a delightful treat.

Chia seeds are useful in smoothie bowls as a thickening agent or as a healthy topping. Chia seeds that have been exposed to liquid take on a texture similar to tapioca and promote healthy digestion.

Coconut

Perhaps the most familiar tropical food, coconut comes in many different forms perfect for smoothie bowls—water, milk, fresh, and dried. Coconut products are high in calcium and potassium as well as protein and plant-based fatty acids. Don't be scared of the high fat content in coconuts; just like avocado, these plant-based fatty acids are actually shown to lower cholesterol and support heart health.

Coconut water is the liquid contained inside the coconut. Coconut water is naturally high in electrolytes and is used by many athletes as a healthy, natural alternative to sugary sports drinks. Coconut water makes a refreshing liquid base for smoothie bowls and is my choice when making a smoothie designed to support recovery from either illness or a workout.

Coconut milk, by contrast, is a milk-like substance made by puréeing the white inner flesh of a coconut with water and straining out the solids. The thicker, fatty part of coconut milk is called coconut cream and is present in canned coconut milk but not the type sold in cartons. Coconut milks in cans and cartons have two very different textures—full-fat canned coconut milk (sometimes referred to as culinary coconut milk) tends to be thick and creamy, requiring a full minute or more of shaking before opening the can to be sure the fatty parts are well incorporated. This tendency for the fat to float to the surface can be used to your advantage, and some recipes will ask you to refrigerate a can of coconut milk to encourage the fat to float to the top and then scrape off the cream to add to your smoothie. Beware of canned coconut milks that contain additives such a sweeteners and thickening agents—the best coconut milks will contain only coconut and water. My favorite canned coconut milk is from Whole Foods' 365 Everyday Value brand of organic coconut milk, as I find it has a superior texture and flavor to other brands I have tried.

Coconut milk in cartons is thinner and easily pourable, making it a good substitute for dairy milk in recipes and on cereal. Most cartoned coconut milks will contain emulsifiers and other additives that help maintain the smooth texture of the milk. Which additives are in your coconut milk is particularly important if you are following a Paleo or Whole 30 diet, so be sure to read your labels. If you can't find a carton of coconut milk that works for your dietary restrictions, all the recipes in this book that use coconut milk will also blend up delightfully with canned coconut milk.

Coconut flesh is also delicious fresh! If you are unable to find fresh coconuts locally, you can order them online from several websites, including Amazon. To prepare a fresh coconut, start by poking a hole in one of the "eyes" with a small, sharp knife or wine corkscrew. Pour the coconut water out of the coconut through the hole and into a glass. Drink or save the water in the fridge to use in a smoothie bowl recipe later. Next, you'll need to crack the coconut open. To do this, imagine the eyes are the north pole and hit around the perimeter of the "equator" with the *back* of a heavy knife or hit it against the edge of a concrete step. Continue hitting it where the "equator" is, rotating it to hit it in a different spot on the equator until the coconut naturally cracks in half. Remove the white flesh from the shell by inserting a spoon or a paring knife between the shell and the membrane surrounding the white flesh and pry away the pieces. Use the paring knife to scrape the brown membrane away. This process may sound tedious, but it's easier than you might think. Freshly cracked coconut halves also make fun natural bowls!

How to Crack Open a Fresh Coconut

Fresh coconut is a fun ingredient to incorporate into your smoothie bowl repertoire. Cracking open a fresh coconut is easy but can feel overwhelming if you have never done it before. Follow these instructions for a perfect crack every time!

1. Start by poking a hole in one of the "eyes" with a small, sharp knife or wine corkscrew. Pour the coconut water out of the coconut through the hole and into a glass. Drink or save the water in the fridge to use in a smoothie bowl.
2. To split the coconut in half, hold the coconut as if the eyes are the north pole and hit around the perimeter of the "equator" with the back of a heavy knife or hit it against the edge of a concrete step. Continue hitting it where the "equator" is, rotating it to hit it in a different spot on the equator until the coconut naturally cracks in half.
3. Remove the white flesh from the shell of one half by inserting a spoon or a paring knife between the shell and the membrane surrounding the white flesh and prying away pieces.

Are you a visual person? Visit my YouTube channel, *Creative Green Living*, for a step-by-step tutorial teaching you how to crack open a coconut.

Coconut is also available in several dried forms, and I encourage you to experiment with different brands to find one you like. The texture and flavors of dried coconut can change drastically depending on how it is prepared. Be sure to check the ingredients label if you are avoiding added sugars or preservatives.

Dragon Fruit/Pitaya

Dragon fruit, also known as pitaya, looks a bit like a science fiction writer's interpretation of what a dragon egg might look like. Most dragon fruit are pink with green scales, though yellow skinned varieties do exist. The flesh inside is either white or dark pink with hundreds of tiny black seeds. The seeds are soft and edible like the seeds inside a kiwi, and the mild, sweet flavor has been described as a combination between a pear and a kiwi.

Dragon fruit are grown in warm, humid regions like Central and South America as well as in Southeast Asia. The dragon fruit industry in both California and Florida is growing, but for the most part, pitaya that you find in the store will come from overseas. The climate where I live in Oregon is not well suited for growing pitaya, but if you live in a warm humid region, definitely try growing a pitaya plant in your yard for easy access to this tropical superfruit!

Dragon fruit is a good source of iron, magnesium, and calcium, as well as vitamins B-2 and C. The edible seeds are high in both omega-3 and omega-6 fatty acids that support your cardiovascular health. All types of pitaya are rich in free radical–fighting antioxidants, though they are more abundant in the pink-fleshed variety.

To prepare fresh dragon fruit, cut the fruit in half lengthwise and peel away the thick, outer flesh with your hands the same way you might with an avocado skin. You can also use a spoon to scoop out the flesh—similar to how you might eat a kiwi—but I find the peeling method to be the most efficient and least wasteful. The outer shell isn't edible, but it does make a fun natural bowl to serve a fruit salad or smoothie bowl in! You can also find pitaya in the frozen foods section both in cubes as well as puréed "smoothie packs." Beware—fresh pink-fleshed dragon fruit will stain your hands, cutting board, and anything it touches, just like a beet would. For this reason, many people prefer the white-fleshed variety for fresh eating and buy pink-fleshed pitaya already prepared and frozen.

Flaxseeds

If an award were given for "longest running tenure as a superfood," flaxseed would win by a long shot. Flaxseeds have a long history dating back to ancient Babylon, where it was cultivated for its health benefits. More than five thousand years later and the flaxseed industry is still going strong!

Flaxseed is high in omega-3 fatty acids, fiber, protein, manganese, magnesium, phosphorus, selenium, and antioxidants. One of the antioxidants specific to flaxseeds, lignans, are thought to support cancer recovery, diabetes management, and reduce inflammation. In fact, flaxseeds have more lignans than any other food!

Flaxseed is an easy way to add a nutritional boost to smoothies, as it is flavorless once blended. To take advantage of flaxseed's nutritional benefits, be sure to use ground flaxseed. You can grind the flaxseeds before putting them in your smoothie, or add them whole if your blender will grind them up for you during the smoothie-making process. If flaxseeds are not ground before eating, they're likely to pass through your intestinal tract without being digested—which means your body isn't able to take advantage of their nutritional benefits. While you can buy pre-ground flaxseed, buying them whole and grinding before use helps maintain their nutritional integrity. If you pre-grind large batches of flaxseed, store it in a bag in your freezer to prevent nutrient loss through oxidation. Whole flaxseeds should be kept in a cool place like your refrigerator or a cool pantry until ready to use.

Ginger

Delicious and spicy, ginger is a rhizome grown underground that packs a flavorful punch. Gingerols, the components in ginger responsible for its distinct flavor, also inhibit the growth of cancer cells and reduce inflammation. Ginger supports your digestive system by reducing symptoms of indigestion and nausea—which many pregnant moms find particularly helpful when struggling with morning sickness (or "all-day sickness" as was the case with my pregnancies).

When buying ginger, choose fresh ginger root instead of dried or ground ginger whenever possible. To prepare ginger for use in recipes, cut a chunk off the root and remove the thin peel by scraping it with a spoon or cutting it away with a paring knife. Once peeled, ginger can be diced, crushed, or sliced—or simply added to your blender to be blended in with the rest of the smoothie ingredients.

Ginger adds a delicious spice to recipes, and a little goes a long way. If you bought more ginger than you can use in smoothies, try adding it sliced to filtered water along with a sprig of mint or organic lemon slices for a delicious and healthy infused water.

Goji Berries

Although goji berries have been consumed in China for centuries, they are a relatively new phenomenon to the western foodie movement. The bright orangey-red berries can be eaten fresh, juiced, or dried—although dried berries, with a texture similar to raisins, are the easiest to find at North American grocers.

Goji berries are high in antioxidants, vitamins A, B2, and C, as well as selenium, potassium, iron, and calcium. They're often consumed to help boost the immune system as well as support eye health and good digestion. Goji berries are used in Chinese medicine to treat high blood pressure, diabetes, and mood disorders like depression and anxiety. Be aware, though, that goji berries have been known to interact adversely with some pharmaceuticals used for treating those same diseases, so be sure to check with your doctor if you take any medications on a regular basis before incorporating goji berries into your diet.

Since you're most likely to find goji berries in their dried form, very little preparation is needed—just open the bag and add them as a topping to your favorite smoothie bowl! While goji berries do not appear in any of the smoothie recipes in this book (only as a topping), you can soak dry goji berries in water and then add the soaked berries and extra water to your smoothie base for a nutritional boost.

Green Tea and Matcha

Green tea's main claim to superfood fame is its catechin content. Catechins are antioxidants known to fight cell damage, lower cholesterol, lower blood pressure, and support overall cardiovascular health. Green tea also contains an amino acid called L-theanine, which has anti-anxiety effects and increases dopamine. L-theanine is thought to interact synergistically with the low levels of caffeine in the tea to improve brain function without the jitteriness of coffee.

Green tea is commonly thought to increase metabolism and physical performance, but the jury is still out on the accuracy of these claims since not enough studies have been done to confirm this. What studies have agreed on, though, is that regularly consuming green tea lowers your risk of cardiovascular disease as well as your total cholesterol and LDL cholesterol (often called "bad cholesterol") levels.

Matcha, a ground green tea powder, is seeing its time in the nutritional spotlight. Matcha contains all the nutritional benefits listed above, but because you actually consume the powdered green tea leaves (as opposed to brewing and then discarding the leaves), you receive more nutrients cup for cup versus brewed tea. Preparing matcha tea at home is a bit of a process, involving a specialized whisk. Lucky for you, matcha is also ideal for blending directly into smoothies without any other prep.

Some of the recipes in this book will call for using brewed green tea. Green tea can be brewed in water that is just below boiling or cold-brewed. While all green tea is beneficial, the less processed the tea is before it gets to you, the better. This means that whole leaf, organic green tea is preferable to ground tea in bags. When brewing tea, use filtered water if you can to avoid chlorine and fluoride in your tea. Pour 8 ounces of hot or cold water over 1 teaspoon of tea leaves (or one tea bag). If using hot water, strain out the leaves after 3 minutes. For cold brew green tea, allow the tea to steep for 4 to 6 hours before straining. I like to keep brewed green tea on hand in my fridge for smoothies as well as drinking throughout the day. You can also brew the tea immediately before blending by pouring just 4 ounces of hot water over 1 teaspoon of loose tea or one teabag, steeping for 3 minutes, and then immediately pouring it over a cup of ice.

Both brewed green tea and matcha add an herbal, earthy flavor to smoothies. If you don't enjoy the strong flavor, it can be easily masked by blending green tea with stronger flavors like berries and pineapple.

Honey

Honey is a sweet superfood that can prevent cancer and heart disease as well as soothe acute sore throats and coughs. All honey is high in antioxidants—although the quantity of antioxidants varies based on the kind of flowers that provided the food source for the bees who made the honey. As a general rule, the darker the color of the honey, the higher its antioxidant content.

There's been some sad news about honey, though. In 2015, researchers from Boston University and Abraxis LLC ran tests on honey samples that showed widespread glyphosate contamination. Glyphosate, the active ingredient in herbicides like Round Up, has been labeled by the World Health Organization as a probable carcinogen and is the anti-superfood—basically, it's straight-up poison and definitely *not* something you should knowingly expose yourself to.

Even though some organic honeys were also found to be contaminated with glyphosate in the study, organic honey was much less likely to be contaminated, and *if* contamination was found, the level of contamination was lower than the contamination level in conventional honey samples tested. To source the healthiest honey possible, stick with organic honey. If possible, go visit the honey vendors at your local farmers' market and talk to them about their honey farming practices.

Kale

Wondering what the hype about kale is? Well, just 1 cup of chopped kale has 684 percent of your RDA of vitamin K, 206 percent RDA of vitamin A, and 134 percent vitamin C—that's a lot of vitamins packed into one little cup! Kale doesn't stop there. It's also a good source of manganese, and copper and is one of the most effective vegetables at stopping damage from free radicals.

To prepare fresh kale to use in smoothies, strip the leafy outer edges away from the center stalk. Discard the stalks, and add the leafy bits to your blender. While frozen kale is often available in blocks in the frozen foods aisle, I find that fresh kale blends nicer into smoothies without leaving little green bits behind to get stuck in your teeth. My favorite variety of kale to use in smoothies is lacinato kale, which is also sometimes labeled as dinosaur kale or Tuscan kale—but be sure to experiment with different varieties to find the one you most enjoy.

If kale is grown in soil contaminated with pesticides or heavy metals, it can soak up those contaminants and store them in the leaves, so be sure to pick up organic kale whenever it's available. If you have a home garden, get your garden soil tested for the presence of lead and other heavy metals it you would like to grow your own kale.

Kale can give smoothies a bit of a grassy flavor, although this can be mitigated by pairing kale with another flavor to mask the "green" taste. Try the recipes in this book, and don't be afraid to experiment more on your own to find your favorite flavor combinations. Smoothies made with kale will take on a beautiful, deep green color. For more appealing-colored smoothies, remember the color wheel and try to avoid using red ingredients with kale so the resulting smoothie is not brown.

Kiwi

Despite their odd exterior appearance, the delicious green flesh of the kiwi gives a delightfully sweet and tart flavor to smoothies as both an ingredient and a topping.

Cup-for-cup, kiwi has five times more vitamin C than an orange—clocking in at 273 percent of your RDA. Though nowhere near the impressive quantity contained in kale, kiwi is also high in vitamin K, with 1 cup of kiwi providing 89 percent of your RDA. Kiwi are also great sources of vitamins A, B6, and E as well as free radical-fighting antioxidants.

When shopping, select kiwi that are firm or that only have a small amount of give. Soft kiwi will be mealy and not taste as good as a properly ripened fruit. Conventionally grown kiwi does not register high for persistent pesticides, so if you're trying to save money on your grocery bill, you can buy non-organic kiwi with a clear conscience!

To prepare kiwi for recipes or fresh eating, peel away the brown fuzzy skin with a serrated peeler and drop in the blender or cut up as desired. Alternatively, you can cut a kiwi in half widthwise and use a spoon to scoop the green flesh out the brown skin—although I find this method to be more wasteful than the first.

Because of their firm texture, kiwi make great candidates for cutting out fun shapes to make garnishes. To do this, try peeling a kiwi and then cutting into quarter-inch thick slices. Next, use small cookie cutters or a small knife to cut out shapes like hearts and stars.

Kiwi will add a delightfully tart flavor to smoothies and pairs particularly well with other green smoothie ingredients—due to both color compatibility and having a complementary flavor.

Kombucha

Enjoyable on its own, kombucha makes an excellent superfood smoothie ingredient. Kombucha is a sweetened tea fermented with a SCOBY (symbiotic colony of bacteria and yeast), which eats the sugar and leaves the tea lightly carbonated and full of beneficial enzymes, probiotics, and B vitamins. Kombucha is available in unflavored varieties, and it is very common to flavor kombucha with different fruits and herbs. These natural flavors aren't usually enough to impart a significant nutritional boost to the kombucha—but it sure does taste good!

Kombucha supports your body's natural detoxification processes and promotes healthy digestion due to the high probiotic content. This high probiotic content has also been credited with improving symptoms of both depression and anxiety.

Kombucha is widely available pre-bottled in grocery and health-food stores. For $2 to $5 a pint, though, the price can add up if you drink a lot of it. If you're an avid consumer of kombucha, you may want to consider brewing your own! For detailed instructions on how to brew your own kombucha, see *The Big Book of Kombucha* by Hannah Crum (2016, Storey) or for a guide to not just creating great kombucha but other beneficial fermented beverages, check out *Delicious Probiotic Drinks* by Julia Mueller (2014, Skyhorse).

The flavor profile of kombucha will vary widely from brand to brand. If you don't like your first interaction with kombucha, don't give up! Try another brand or a different flavor. Still not your favorite? The recipes in this book are a great way to get the probiotic and nutritional benefits of kombucha without having to drink it straight (thereby avoiding the flavor some may consider too strong).

Mango

A vitamin C powerhouse (one mango contains more than 200 percent of your RDA!), mango is also high in vitamins A and B-6, as well as potassium, folate, and magnesium. Just like all our other superfoods, mango is high in antioxidants. One antioxidant prolific in mango, zeaxanthin, filters out harmful blue light rays and is thought to help protect eyes from age-related damage and diseases like macular degeneration. Other antioxidants in mango are thought to fight both free-radicals and cancer cells.

To ensure a ripe mango, choose one with slight give that isn't soft or squishy. Mangos come in many colors so the color of the peel is not an indicator of ripeness—definitely get your hands on the fruit! If you accidentally buy a mango that is too firm, you can leave it on your counter at room temperature to allow it to continue to ripen as you would with a too-green banana. Prepared mango is also available in bags in the freezer section of your grocery store. While choosing organic is always a great idea, mango is one of the least pesticide-contaminated fruits, making conventional mango a good choice to help save money in your food budget.

To prepare fresh mango for smoothies, peel it with a serrated peeler and cut the flesh away from the center pit with a knife. You could also cut the mango in half, away from the pit, without peeling, and then make cuts in a grid pattern that cut through the flesh but not the skin. Push on the back of skin to make the mango squares pop in a fun pattern perfect for serving alongside your smoothie bowl.

Nuts

While nuts are universally high in protein, fatty acids, minerals, and vitamins, some have their own unique super powers. Walnuts are particularly high in omega-3 fatty acids. Almonds are high in manganese and magnesium. Brazil nuts contain extraordinary levels of selenium. Some doctors even prescribe Brazil nuts to their patients instead of synthetic selenium supplements as part of their thyroid disease management plan!

Whether you prefer one style of nut at a time or a blend, nuts make a great smoothie bowl topping. Almonds and raw cashews are often used to top the recipes in this book, but don't be afraid to mix it up! Swap out the nuts in one recipe for a new type of nut or a nut blend. Or try adding nuts where I didn't include any. Whenever I'm looking to add a protein boost to a smoothie bowl or make it more filling, I always add nuts!

Roasted nuts can contain undesirable additives, so raw nuts are the preference of most health-conscious nut fans. Almost all "raw" nuts sold in the USA are pasteurized with steam or another chemical gas. Because the pasteurization method is rarely disclosed on the packaging, choose organic nuts whenever possible to reduce your exposure to undesirable chemicals.

Gluten-free readers beware: while nuts themselves are free of gluten, common additives containing gluten can be added during manufacturing. Nuts can also be processed in facilities that process wheat-containing products, so always read your labels! Recipes labeled gluten-free in this book assume you have chosen nuts free of gluten contaminants if gluten is a dietary concern for you.

When buying nuts in the store, you will pay a premium if you opt for prepared nuts that have been sliced, ground, or chopped for you. If you like to use nuts as a topping on your smoothie bowls, save money and prevent oxidation by purchasing whole nuts and chopping them yourself by pulsing them in a food processor. Store pre-ground or chopped nuts in a mason jar in the freezer to slow down the oxidation process.

Oats

When most people think of oats, they picture a hot bowl of oatmeal or a sweet oatmeal cookie. Though it might sound unconventional, oats actually make a great addition to smoothie bowls! Whether it's through a granola topping or by blending them into the smoothie itself, oats provide bulk (helping you feel full) as well as a big boost of protein, iron, manganese, phosphorus, thiamin, folate, and magnesium. In fact, 1 cup of dry rolled oats contains a whopping 26 grams of protein and 40 percent of your daily recommended intake of iron!

While oats in their pure form do not contain gluten, oats are often grown side-by-side with or processed in facilities where wheat, barley, and rye products are also grown and processed—making the risk for contamination high. Some people who have been advised by their doctors to stop eating gluten may have also been advised to avoid oats. If you're making a smoothie bowl for a gluten-free friend, be sure to ask if they can have oats before preparing a recipe containing granola or rolled oats.

Those sensitive to gluten should always make sure to use certified gluten-free oats and granola to be confident these products have not been contaminated with gluten. Both conventional and gluten-free oats have the potential to be contaminated with glyphosate (remember, this is the active ingredient in commercial weed killers like Round Up), so I always try to purchase organic oats.

Oats don't impart a distinct color or flavor to smoothies, making them a flexible ingredient that can be added to most smoothies that also contain yogurt or plant milk (I do not recommend them as an ingredient in nice cream). If you're looking for an easy way to increase your protein and iron intake, add a quarter cup of rolled oats to your morning smoothie bowl—your tastebuds probably won't even notice!

Oranges

Oranges are famous for their vitamin C content, but the benefits of oranges don't stop there—oranges are also high in fiber, folate, and a host of free radical–fighting antioxidants. Of course, they are also that brilliant orange color, which nicely complements other orange smoothie ingredients like carrots, mango, and peaches both in color and flavor.

To get the maximum nutritional benefit from oranges in your smoothies, use fresh oranges rather than pre-squeezed orange juice. Because vitamin C degrades quickly when exposed to oxygen, shortening the length of time between juicing the orange and adding it to your smoothie will help you get more nutritional bang for your buck. Using orange segments instead of orange juice also boosts the amount of fiber in your smoothie, helping support healthy digestion.

If it isn't practical to use fresh oranges for your smoothies instead of juice, be sure to look for orange juice produced in the United States. This is because the fungicide, carbendazim—which is banned in the United States—has been found in orange juice imported from other countries such as Brazil. If your OJ is imported from Canada, don't assume that Canada and the United States are similar enough that it won't matter. Canada doesn't grow its own oranges, so any juice imported from Canada came from oranges grown in other countries where carbendazim may have been permitted.

Peaches

Sweet and juicy, peaches are not just round, but a well-*rounded* source of vitamins and minerals. While they can't boast RDA percentages in the hundreds like many of the superfoods on this list, peaches contain many different vitamins and minerals in moderate amounts—which makes them a great all-around healthy food. Peaches are good sources of vitamins A, C, E, K, and a host of B vitamins. They're also a good way to get fiber, potassium, and omega-6 fatty acids in your diet.

For the most nutritional benefit, choose fresh or frozen peaches. Although they're delicious, canned peaches often have added sugar and preservatives. The heat used in the canning process destroys some of the nutrients contained in the fresh peaches, as well. If the peaches were canned in metal cans (as opposed to glass jars), there's a high likelihood that the peaches absorbed BPA and other hormone-disrupting phthalates from the can lining. Freezing, on the other hand, preserves many of the nutrients destroyed by heat processing and avoids the hormone disrupting chemicals found in cans.

Due to the high level of persistent pesticide residues found on conventionally grown peaches, opt for organic peaches whenever they're available. If you aren't able to find organic peaches, wash them well and peel them with a serrated peeler to help mitigate your exposure to pesticides sprayed on the peaches while in the orchard.

Peaches will give your smoothies a fresh, sweet taste and beautiful yellow-orange color. The color is mild enough, though that it can easily be masked by red, green, and purple ingredients without turning your smoothie brown, so don't be afraid to experiment with this delicious fruit.

Pineapple

Near the end of my pregnancy with my second child, I ate bowl after bowl of fresh pineapple, as an old wives' tale claims it will help put you into labor if your baby and body are ready to go. It didn't work. It did, however, give me a great boost of both vitamin C and manganese—just 1 cup of fresh pineapple chunks will get you 131 percent of your RDA of vitamins C and 76 percent of your RDA of manganese.

As one of the fruits with the lowest pesticide contamination, don't be afraid to pick up conventional pineapple if organic pineapple isn't available. One thing you should always avoid, though, is pineapple in cans. Not only does canned pineapple taste bad, but because the lining in metal food cans contain endocrine-disrupting phthalates like BPA and BPS, the fruit will be contaminated with these chemicals, as well.

To choose the perfect fresh pineapple, look for a pineapple that feels heavy for its size and smells sweet—avoid any that smell musty. To prepare it, cut off the top and bottom then stand it on end to cut away the bumpy outer skin. Cut out the tough, fibery core by using a coring tool or by cutting the fruit into wedges and then cutting away the point. If that sounds like too much work, frozen pineapple is inexpensive and available year-round!

Pineapple will give your smoothies a bright, tangy flavor. The mild, yellow color combines well with other smoothie bowl ingredients without imparting a strong hue. This makes pineapple an especially versatile fruit for using in a variety of smoothies.

Raspberries

Available in both red and black varieties, raspberries are a sweet treat I look forward to every summer. Red raspberries are the most common, but black raspberries are growing in popularity. If your local grocer doesn't carry fresh black raspberries in the summer or autumn when they're in season, try looking in the frozen fruit aisle—you might be surprised to find them there!

Red and black raspberries have a similar nutrition profile in regard to their vitamin and mineral content. Where black raspberries really steal the spotlight, though, is with their antioxidant count. Black raspberries have more than ten times the number of antioxidants—especially anthocyanins—than red raspberries. Responsible for black raspberries' signature color, anthocyanins are powerful antioxidants that can both fight and prevent cancer.

Look for fresh organic raspberries of both colors in stores and farmers' markets in summer. Due to their ability to readily absorb pesticides, be sure to stick with organic berries. Frozen raspberries are another great way to buy berries to incorporate into your diet year-round. Raspberries will give either a red or purple hue (depending on which variety you use) to your smoothies along with a sweet and slightly tart flavor.

Spinach

Turns out Popeye really was on to something! Spinach is a great source of vitamins A and C as well as blood cell–building iron. If canned spinach or big salads aren't your thing, smoothie bowls are a great way to get more spinach into your system.

With a mild flavor, the taste of spinach is easily masked by other foods. You can use it to bring a fun, green punch to a traditionally flavored smoothie like Green-ya Colada (page 158) without making it taste grassy. Spinach's mild flavor also makes it a parent's secret weapon against kids who hate green stuff. You can hide spinach with dark-colored berries in recipes like Morning Matchavation (page 182) and Greenberry (page 209) and your kids will never be the wiser.

When shopping for spinach to use in smoothie bowls, look for fresh organic baby spinach—organic because leafy greens are notorious for holding onto conventional pesticides despite being washed and baby because the tender leaves will blend more readily into the smoothie without large, telltale green bits. Despite Popeye's love for it, skip canned spinach. Frozen spinach works in a pinch, but I find it harder to get the greens to blend nicely.

If you love that pretty green color, don't be afraid to experiment! You can add a handful of spinach to most smoothies—although, you may want to avoid adding it to a red smoothie to keep it from turning a weird shade of brown.

Strawberries

High in vitamin C, fiber, and manganese, these ruby jewels of summer are my favorite part of June. Strawberries have one of the highest concentrations of antioxidants and phenols of any other fruit or vegetable, making strawberries an excellent tool in your food-based cancer- and disease-fighting arsenal.

Strawberries are another food you want to always buy organic. Strawberries take up high levels of persistent pesticides you definitely don't want in your smoothie bowl, and organic farming practices are the best ways to avoid those. Luckily, organic strawberries are increasing in popularity and are usually easy to find at the market.

My favorite strawberries are a variety we have in Oregon called Hood Strawberries. You will probably never find them outside of Oregon farmers' markets. Developed for their flavor and texture, these juicy morsels spoil just a few days after picking, so they aren't suitable for shipping and you can only buy them locally. Why am I telling you this? Because chances are good you have a specialty local strawberry, too! Start asking around at the farmers' market in June and you're sure to encounter strawberries more flavorful than anything you've ever bought in a store!

Stock up on fresh strawberries during the summer and freeze them to use later in the year. To prepare strawberries for freezing, just wash and pat dry as well as remove the green leaves on top. Lay them out in a single layer on a cookie sheet to freeze before adding to a freezer bag for storage. If that's more work than you want to put into your strawberries, you can also pick up prefrozen organic strawberries in the frozen fruit aisle of any grocery store.

Watermelon

I don't know if there is a more quintessential summer food than watermelon. Many people think of watermelon as a low-nutrition fruit comprising mostly sugar and water. While it's true that watermelons are about 90 percent water, they still pack a considerable amount of nutrition per calorie. Watermelon is a good source of omega-6 fatty acids as well as vitamins A and C. Surprisingly, watermelon has more lycopene—a popular antioxidant known for helping reduce ailments common to aging—than a tomato. Watermelon's antioxidant content is rather stable and will remain intact several days after a watermelon has been cut open if stored in the fridge.

To choose a perfectly ripe watermelon, look for a melon that feels heavy for its size and has a yellowish spot on one side where the watermelon was resting on the ground in the field—if a melon is missing this spot, it is likely that it was picked prematurely.

To prepare fresh watermelon, wash the outside of the melon with soapy water to remove dirt and pesticide residue. Next, cut off the blossom and stem ends and stand it cut-side down. Go around the outside of the watermelon and cut away the rind. You will then have a watermelon ready to slice, cube, carve, and more! To freeze watermelon, cut the rindless watermelon into cubes and lay them out on a layer of paper towels. Blot dry with an additional towel and transfer to a cookie sheet. Keep the cookie sheet in the freezer for two hours or more before transferring the cubes to a freezer bag for longer term storage.

Yogurt

Fermented and full of good bacteria, yogurt will give you a hefty dose of probiotics along with calcium and vitamin B-2 as well as omega-3 and omega-6 fatty acids. Yogurt isn't just for the dairy-friendly—vegan yogurts made from coconut, almond, soy, or hemp milks are also widely available and will give you the same probiotic boost as its dairy counterpart.

Both dairy or vegan yogurts will lend a thick, creamy consistency to your smoothie. If you like your smoothie extra creamy, use a Greek-style yogurt. Greek yogurt has been strained to separate more of the whey from the yogurt, leaving the remaining product thicker and with a higher protein density.

If you choose to use dairy yogurt, go for organic. Many sad things are happening in conventional dairy farming including giving cows unnatural GMO feed and treating them with growth hormones (the FDA claims there is no difference between milk produced by cows treated with bovine growth hormones and those that are not). Organic dairy cows, on the other hand, are fed an organic, non-GMO diet and are not treated with bovine growth hormone. Organic milk has the added benefit of being higher in omega-3 fatty acids and lower in pesticide residues than conventional milk—qualities that are passed along when that organic milk is turned into yogurt.

If you choose a vegan yogurt, choose a non-GMO certified yogurt if the base is soymilk. Unless soy is organic or non-GMO certified, it's likely to be grown from GMO seeds and treated with heavy doses of herbicide such as Round Up—definitely not something you want to eat for breakfast! Other common vegan yogurt bases are coconut, hemp, and almond milks, which do not have GMO counterparts.

When buying yogurt, my preference is to purchase unsweetened yogurt. Sweetened yogurts can contain a variety of natural and artificial sweeteners, preservatives, food colorings, and more. By getting plain, unsweetened yogurt, I control what it is sweetened with or if it is sweetened at all.

Blending Our Way Through the Rainbow

As you may have noticed in the previous chapter, superfoods come in a rainbow of colors. To better facilitate the advice to *eat a rainbow every day*, I've organized the following recipes in rainbow order. We'll start with white and light smoothie bowls and move through pink, red, orange, yellow, green, blue, and finally purple!

As you choose new recipes, mix it up! If you have a red smoothie for breakfast, try a green one for snack time. If you ate a purple smoothie bowl yesterday, try a yellow one today. This will help make sure you are getting a wide variety of nutrients for maximum nourishment.

While the quantities of the toppings listed in the recipes will match the photos, don't be afraid to branch out on your own. If you're looking for an extra protein boost, top your bowl with a drizzle of yogurt and a handful of nuts. Want to eat a rainbow in every smoothie bowl? Choose a topping in each color to help give a well-rounded variety. If you ever need ideas for great toppings, flip back through the previous chapter at the list of superfoods for inspiration.

Now, without further ado, let's get blending!

Berries and Cream

Some people don't like color. As a person who loves rainbows, I don't understand this. If you have a color-hater in your life, they don't need to miss out on the benefits of a superfood smoothie, though! This smoothie base has a creamy, vanilla flavor, which is the perfect foundation to help your favorite berry combination shine.

Ingredients

Smoothie Bowl

1 frozen banana

½ cup full-fat coconut milk

½ cup raw cashews

⅛ tsp vanilla extract

Toppings

¼ cup fresh blueberries

¼ cup fresh raspberries

½ cup fresh strawberries, halved

Directions

1. Combine all smoothie bowl ingredients in a blender jar and blend until smooth and no chunks remain.

2. Pour into a bowl and add toppings.

This versatile smoothie base is delicious topped with any combination of fresh seasonal fruit!

Piña Colada

Sammi Ricke, of *Grounded and Surrounded* (groundedandsurrounded.com)

This tropical smoothie bowl will transport you straight to the beaches of the Caribbean! The silky coconut cream contributes to the smooth texture while the addition of protein-packed Greek yogurt will keep you full for hours.

Ingredients

Smoothie Bowl

- ¼ cup coconut cream (skimmed from the top of refrigerated full-fat coconut milk in a can)
- 2 Tbsp full-fat coconut water (from the bottom of the refrigerated can)
- 1 cup frozen pineapple chunks
- ½ cup plain Greek yogurt
- 1 tsp vanilla extract

Toppings

- 1 Tbsp hemp seeds
- 2 Tbsp dried coconut shreds
- 10 fresh cherries, pitted
- ¼ cup pineapple chunks
- ¼ cup kiwi, diced

Directions

1. Combine all smoothie bowl ingredients in a blender jar and blend until smooth and no chunks remain.

2. Pour into a hollowed-out pineapple or a bowl and add toppings.

Chill the can of full-fat coconut milk for at least 6 hours before assembling your smoothie bowl to ensure the white coconut cream solidifies at the top. Gently scoop out the white cream from the top of the can to measure ¼ cup and pour 2 tablespoons of the clear coconut water into your blender. Save the remaining chilled coconut milk for additional smoothie bowls!

Apple Pie

Last summer, Oregon had unseasonably hot weather. After returning home one day with apples from my parents' house, my oldest son asked if we could bake a pie. Since it was 100 degrees outside, I declined. I did, however, offer to make him an apple pie smoothie and it was a hit! This smoothie bowl is perfect for any time of year—not just when the mercury on the thermometer soars.

Ingredients

Smoothie Bowl

2 small apples, peeled and cored
½ cup plain whole milk yogurt
1 Tbsp agave syrup
1 tsp apple pie spice
2 frozen bananas

Toppings

1 large apple slice
1 Tbsp apples, diced
1 Tbsp granola
1 Tbsp yogurt drizzle
dash of cinnamon

Directions

1. Combine all smoothie bowl ingredients in a blender jar and blend until smooth and no chunks remain.

2. Pour into a bowl and add toppings.

To make frozen bananas easier to use, I always break bananas into six pieces before freezing. This makes measuring bananas simple and makes smoothies easier to blend than if you used one large frozen banana.

Fruity Colada

Piña colada is a classic flavor that also makes a great base for other fruity combinations! Peaches and strawberries are two of my favorite flavors to add to a classic piña colada. Using lime-flavored kombucha as part of the smoothie cuts the sweetness and gives a great probiotic boost.

Ingredients

Smoothie Bowl

½ cup frozen pineapple chunks

½ cup frozen peach chunks

½ cup frozen strawberries

½ cup coconut or other
plant-based milk

½ cup lime-flavored kombucha

Toppings

¼ cup fresh blackberries

1 Tbsp dried coconut pieces

lime wedge

Directions

1. Combine all smoothie bowl ingredients in a blender jar and blend until smooth and no chunks remain.

2. Pour into a bowl and add toppings.

Blackberries not in season? Leave frozen berries out on the counter to partially defrost while making the rest of the smoothie bowl and top your bowl with those instead!

Watermelon Dream

V P gf df

Do you love watermelon? I don't think I've met a single person who doesn't! Combining frozen watermelon with fresh (and just a bit of kombucha) turns watermelon into an even more delicious treat reminiscent of a granita or slushy—but with none of the added dye or sugar.

Ingredients

Smoothie Bowl

2½ cups frozen watermelon chunks
1 cup fresh watermelon chunks
½ cup strawberry kombucha

Toppings

sprig of fresh mint
2 blackberries

Directions

1. Combine all smoothie bowl ingredients in a blender jar and blend until smooth and no chunks remain.

2. Pour into a bowl and add toppings.

To help keep watermelon chunks from freezing into a large blob, pat them dry before laying separated chunks on a cookie sheet to freeze. Store in a large zip-top bag once completely frozen.

Banana Berry

Strawberries and bananas go together like peanut butter and jelly. Strawberries aren't the only fruit that make a perfect pair with bananas, though! This smoothie blends strawberries, cherries, and blueberries together with bananas to make a perfectly sweet treat.

Ingredients

Smoothie Bowl

1 banana, peeled

½ cup frozen cherries

½ cup frozen strawberries

½ cup frozen blueberries

¾ cup coconut or other plant-based milk

1 Tbsp flaxseed

Toppings

¼ cup mixed berries

1 Tbsp granola

Directions

1. Combine all smoothie bowl ingredients in a blender jar and blend until smooth and no chunks remain.

2. Pour into a bowl and add toppings.

Tropical Dragon Nice Cream (V) (gf) (df)

Tropical flavors are my favorite partners for dragon fruit. While you can find dragon fruit in both pink and white varieties, my preference is to buy the pink-fleshed kind for this recipe because I love the color!

Ingredients

Smoothie Bowl

1 cup frozen dragon fruit (pitaya) chunks

1 cup frozen pineapple chunks

1 tsp agave syrup

¾ cup strawberry-flavored kombucha

1 frozen banana

½ cup frozen mango chunks

Toppings

1 large strawberry

edible flowers

Directions

1. Combine all smoothie bowl ingredients in a food processor and pulse until smooth, stopping as needed to scrape down the sides.

2. Scoop into a bowl or half coconut and top with a large, fresh strawberry and edible flowers as desired.

For instructions on how to crack a coconut in half to make fun bowls, visit my YouTube channel, Creative Green Living.

Dragonberry

Both pink- and white-fleshed pitaya taste like a kiwi/pear hybrid that mixes well with other tropical fruits. The pink-fleshed variety is also easy to find in the frozen fruit section of your grocery store and lends a beautiful, brilliant color to this smoothie recipe.

Ingredients

Smoothie Bowl

- ½ cup frozen dragon fruit (pitaya) chunks
- ½ cup frozen peach chunks
- ½ cup frozen strawberries
- ½ cup frozen mango chunks
- 1 cup coconut water

Toppings

- 2 Tbsp shredded coconut
- Optional: Serve with 1 cup fresh blackberries on the side

Directions

1. Combine all smoothie bowl ingredients in a blender jar and blend until smooth and no chunks remain.

2. Pour into a bowl and top with coconut. Serve with 1 cup fresh blackberries on the side, if desired.

Look for frozen dragon fruit or pitaya in the frozen fruit aisle at the grocery store or buy a fresh dragon fruit and scoop out the inner flesh, cut into chunks, and freeze. If using a fresh pink flesh dragon fruit, beware that it is likely to stain!

Teaberry

When I worked at a coffee shop in college, my favorite thing on the menu at the time was a blended drink that was a combination of tea and berries. To make it extra sinful, you could add a bit of cream to the blender, too! This bowl is inspired by my college coffee shop favorite but made healthier by removing the sugar and switching to plant-based ingredients.

Ingredients

Smoothie Bowl

- 2 cups frozen strawberries
- ½ cup fresh or frozen pomegranate arils
- 1 cup full-fat coconut milk
- ½ cup brewed green tea, chilled

Toppings

- ¼ cup blueberries
- 2 Tbsp shredded coconut

Directions

1. Combine all smoothie bowl ingredients in a blender jar and blend until smooth and no chunks remain.

2. Pour into a bowl and add toppings.

Try substituting kombucha for the green tea in this recipe for a probiotic boost!

Something Pink Please
V P gf df

It's easy to accidentally find yourself in a food rut. After a blitz of green smoothie experiments, my son asked if I could make him "something pink, please!" We keep our freezer well stocked with an assortment of frozen fruit so I was more than happy to oblige with a strawberry- and cherry-based wonder—finished with a cherry on top!

Ingredients

Smoothie Bowl

1½ cups frozen strawberries
½ cup frozen dark cherries
½ cup frozen pineapple
1¼ cup coconut water

Toppings

1 small banana, peeled and sliced
⅓ cup blueberries
1 fresh cherry with stem

Directions

1. Combine all smoothie bowl ingredients in a blender jar and blend until smooth and no chunks remain.

2. Pour into a bowl and add toppings.

Millions of Peaches

V P gf df

If you've considered moving to the country to eat a lot of peaches, this recipe is for you. Don't use peaches from a can, though—use frozen peaches for the smoothie and then top it with a sliced fresh peach. It's nature's candy!

Ingredients

Smoothie Bowl

1 banana, peeled

1 Tbsp flaxseed

2 Tbsp raw pumpkin seeds

1 cup frozen peach chunks

½ cup frozen raspberries

¾ cup coconut or other plant-based milk

Toppings

½ peach, sliced

1 tsp chia seeds

Directions

1. Combine all smoothie bowl ingredients in a blender jar and blend until smooth and no chunks remain.

2. Pour into a bowl and add toppings.

Keep flaxseed fresh after opening the bag by storing the sealed bag in the refrigerator.

Peachy Pom

When summer hits, fresh fruit is king! Fresh peaches and berries are abundant and perfect for smoothie bowls. Pop some of your "U-pick" goodies in the freezer (don't forget to peel and cut up peaches first) to turn into smoothies. Be sure to leave some fresh fruit unfrozen for toppings!

Ingredients

Smoothie Bowl

- 1 cup frozen peach chunks
- ¼ cup fresh or frozen pomegranate arils
- ¼ cup frozen blueberries
- ¾ cup coconut or other plant-based milk

Toppings

- ½ banana, peeled and sliced
- ¼ cup blueberries
- ¼ cup granola

Directions

1. Combine all smoothie bowl ingredients in a blender jar and blend until smooth and no chunks remain.

2. Pour into a bowl and add toppings. Serve with fresh cherries on the side, if desired.

> If fresh pomegranates aren't in season, look for frozen pomegranate arils in the frozen fruit aisle at your local grocery store.

Creamy Cherry Berry Booster
gf

Do you love the taste of fresh cream or yogurt with berries? I sure do! This smoothie bowl combines the taste of strawberries and cherries with smooth, creamy yogurt and coconut milk. Serve it in a mason jar with visible banana slices for a fun twist!

Ingredients

Smoothie Bowl

1 cup frozen strawberries

1 cup frozen dark cherries

1 Tbsp local honey

½ cup plain whole milk yogurt

1 Tbsp flaxseed

½ cup coconut or other plant-based milk

Toppings

½ banana, sliced thin lengthwise

¼ cup fresh blueberries

¼ cup fresh strawberries, halved

1 tsp shredded coconut

1 Tbsp plain whole milk yogurt

drizzle of honey

Directions

1. Combine all smoothie bowl ingredients in a blender jar and blend until smooth and no chunks remain.

2. Press banana slices against the side of a mason jar before pouring the smoothie into the jar. Add remaining toppings.

Cherry Cobbler

Abbey Sharp, RD, of *Abbey's Kitchen* (abbeyskitchen.com)

This dairy-free, gluten-free smoothie bowl offers the flavors of your favorite summer dessert without the guilt. Ripe, sweet cherries are puréed with wholesome oats and baking spices to yield a healthy cherry cobbler in a bowl.

Ingredients

Smoothie Bowl

- 2 Tbsp rolled oats
- 1 tsp flaxseed
- ½ frozen banana
- 1½ cups cherries
- ¼ cup unsweetened almond or other plant-based milk
- ¼ cup coconut yogurt
- 2 dates, pits removed
- pinch nutmeg
- ¼ tsp cinnamon
- ¼ tsp vanilla extract

Toppings

- ¼ cup whole pecans
- ½ tsp hemp hearts
- 2 Tbsp granola
- 3 fresh cherries, pitted and halved
- ½ tsp cacao nibs
- 1 small banana, peeled and sliced

Directions

1. Combine all smoothie bowl ingredients in a blender jar and blend until smooth and no chunks remain.

2. Pour into a bowl and add toppings.

If you are not sensitive to dairy, you could easily swap in Greek yogurt and dairy milk.
If you're gluten sensitive, be sure to look for both gluten-free rolled oats and gluten-free granola.

Berry Best

While my kids are often the catalysts and inspiration for my many smoothie creations, this one is dedicated to my niece, Heidi, my "berry best," real-food loving niece. Once, as a young child, she turned down an offer of cake at my mom's fiftieth birthday party and asked if she could have more vegetables instead! Cheers to you, Heidi Bear! May your love of plant-based foods grow with each passing year.

Ingredients

Smoothie Bowl

3 Tbsp rolled oats

1 Tbsp chia seeds

1 Tbsp flaxseed

1 cup coconut water

1 Tbsp local honey

¾ cup frozen blueberries

¾ cup frozen strawberries

½ cup frozen peach chunks

Toppings

2 fresh clementines or mandarin oranges, peeled and segmented

½ cup frozen blueberries

1 Tbsp chia seeds

Directions

1. Combine all smoothie bowl ingredients in a blender jar and blend until smooth and no chunks remain.

2. Pour into a bowl and add toppings.

If you don't have a high-powered blender, start by first blending the oats, chia, flaxseed, and coconut water before adding the rest of the ingredients.

Coconut Raspberry Cooler ^{gf} ^{df}

Landen McBride of *Measure and Whisk* (measureandwhisk.com)

Raspberries have a tendency to be a bit sour if they're not perfectly ripe. The addition of sweet cherries balances out any tartness and gives it a mildly sweet and complex flavor. A true "breakfast of champions."

Ingredients

Smoothie Bowl

- 1 can full-fat coconut milk
- 2 cups frozen raspberries
- 1 cup frozen sweet cherries
- 1 tsp fresh lime zest
- ¼ cup cold water
- 1 tsp local honey (optional)

Toppings

- ¼ cup granola
- 2 Tbsp toasted pepitas (pumpkin seeds)
- 2 tsp raw millet
- ½ kiwi, peeled and sliced

Directions

1. Combine all smoothie bowl ingredients in a blender jar and blend until smooth and no chunks remain.

2. Pour into a bowl and add toppings.

Bright Berry Açaí

Sara Welch of *Dinner at the Zoo* (dinneratthezoo.com)

This thick and creamy smoothie bowl is made with fruit, açaí berry purée, and Greek yogurt that's finished with a fun and colorful variety of toppings. Açaí berry purée can be found in the freezer area, typically with the frozen fruit or frozen juices.

Ingredients

Smoothie Bowl

- 1 cup almond milk
- 1 large banana, peeled
- 1½ cups frozen mixed berries
- ½ cup plain Greek yogurt
- 1 Tbsp local honey (or more to taste)
- 1 frozen packet of açaí berry purée (100 grams), broken into pieces

Toppings

- ½ cup fresh berries such as raspberries, blueberries, and strawberries
- 1 Tbsp chia seeds
- 2 Tbsp shaved coconut
- 2 Tbsp sliced almonds
- 1 mint sprig (optional)

Directions

1. Combine all smoothie bowl ingredients in a blender jar and blend until smooth and no chunks remain.

2. Pour into a bowl and add toppings.

If you can't find frozen açaí berry purée, try to look for dried açaí powder. To use powder instead of purée, use 1 teaspoon of the powder plus an additional ½ cup of frozen berries.

Pretty in Pitaya

Caroline Ginolfi of *Plant Based Blonde* (plantbasedblonde.com)

This bowl is sweet, creamy, and beautiful! Oh, that vibrant pink color—it just never gets old.

Ingredients

Smoothie Bowl

2 bananas, peeled

1 cup frozen strawberries

½ cup dragon fruit (pitaya), peeled—about half of a fresh pitaya

¼ cup full-fat coconut milk

Toppings

¼ cup strawberries, chopped

¼ cup blueberries

6 blackberries

¼ cup mango, chopped

1 tsp shredded coconut

Directions

1. Combine all smoothie bowl ingredients in a blender jar and blend until smooth and no chunks remain.

2. Pour into a bowl and add toppings.

Because fresh pitaya is often hard to find year-round, I will buy up a whole bunch when I do find it in the summer, blend the center portion, and freeze in jars so I can enjoy pitaya bowls all year!

To get a thicker "nice cream" texture, use frozen bananas and pitaya instead of fresh.

Kombucha Cherry Chiller

Katherine Mae Stanley of *Nourishing Simplicity* (nourishingsimplicity.org)

This smoothie is bursting with hidden health boosters like gelatin and beetroot powder. You will be hard pressed to detect either when they're blended with creamy coconut, sweet mango, and tart cherries. Cherry kombucha is used in place of water for an extra punch of cherry and dairy-free probiotics. If you chose not to use kombucha, coconut water works well as a substitute!

Ingredients

Smoothie Bowl

- 2 Tbsp unflavored gelatin (collagen hydrolysate)
- 2 tsp beetroot powder
- ½ cup cherry-flavored kombucha
- ¼ cup full-fat coconut milk
- 1 cup frozen tart cherries
- ¾ cup frozen mango chunks

Toppings

- 3 fresh mango, thinly sliced
- 1 fresh cherry
- 1 tsp shredded coconut

Directions

1. Add the gelatin, beet powder, and liquids to blender. Blend for 5 seconds until combined.

2. Add the cherries and mango, blending until smooth and no chunks remain.

3. Pour smoothie into a bowl and add toppings.

Gelatin (collagen hydrolysate) is a flavorless way to add protein and essential nutrients to a smoothie. It promotes a healthy immune system, digestive tract, hair, skin, and nails. Unlike other gelatin types, collagen hydrolysate dissolves in cold liquid.

Pink Kisses

Sara Jansson, on Instagram as @SwimYogaRun

To me, healthy food is food that makes you happy because it looks beautiful, tastes delicious, and is also good for your body. This smoothie combines all three: you become happy by just looking at its vibrant color, it tastes heavenly, and the superfoods beetroot and ginger are great for your body!

Ingredients

Smoothie Bowl

- 1 cup almond milk
- 1 frozen banana
- 1 cup frozen raspberries
- ½ raw beetroot, peeled
- 1-inch fresh ginger, peeled

Toppings

- 3 blackberries
- ¼ cup popped quinoa
- 2 pieces persimmon
- 2 slices yellow beet
- dried edible flowers, to taste

Directions

1. Combine all smoothie bowl ingredients in a blender jar and blend until smooth and no chunks remain.

2. Pour into a bowl and add toppings.

Use small cookie cutters to create stars or other shapes of fruit like I did to the persimmon in the picture. It makes your bowl even prettier and brings a smile to your face!

Enchanted Summer Dream

(V) (gf) (df)

Maja Redlin, on Instagram as @majardln

This smoothie bowl will turn your normal day into an enchanted day. No matter if you eat it during summer or give it a try during winter, this smoothie will animate body and soul and give you the perfect start into your day! It's full of important nutrients and is a great energy source to enchant your morning into a summer dream.

Ingredients

Smoothie Bowl

1 banana, peeled
1 apple, peeled and cored
¾ cup frozen strawberries
½ cup frozen raspberries
½ cup frozen blueberries
1 date, pitted
1 Tbsp chia seeds
1 Tbsp agave syrup
1 tsp flaxseed oil

Toppings

1 Tbsp ground coconut
1 tsp dried, sweetened cranberries
2 Tbsp blueberries
1 strawberry, sliced
¼ cup mixed nuts

Directions

1. Combine all smoothie bowl ingredients in a blender jar and blend until smooth and no chunks remain.

2. Pour into a bowl and add toppings.

Kind of a Fig Deal (V) (gf) (df)

Fresh figs are a seasonal treat you may not be familiar with. If trying new things is scary for you, there's no need to be intimidated! The humble fig makes a great smoothie ingredient or topping. Just pop off the stem and cut it up to top a smoothie bowl or throw it in the blender whole (they are also great to eat fresh!).

Ingredients

Smoothie Bowl

½ banana, peeled

¾ cup frozen peach chunks

½ cup frozen raspberries

1 Tbsp raw pumpkin seeds

2 fresh figs, stems removed

1 cup coconut or other plant-based milk

Toppings

1 fig, cut into wedges

¼ cup granola

Directions

1. Combine all smoothie bowl ingredients in a blender jar and blend until smooth and no chunks remain.

2. Pour into a bowl and top with fig wedges and granola.

Look for fresh figs in late summer or early fall. In some niche markets, you may be able to find them frozen year-round!

Berry Avocado Bliss

V P gf df

Sarah Romero & Elizabeth Menlove of *Kiwi and Carrot* (kiwiandcarrot.com)

This sweet bowl combines frozen berries, almond milk, and avocado for a thick and creamy frozen treat! Top it with kiwi, fresh berries, coconut, and superfood seeds for an added crunch.

Ingredients

Smoothie Bowl

½ cup almond milk

½ frozen banana

1½ cups frozen mixed berries

¼ ripe avocado

Toppings

1 kiwi, peeled

½ Tbsp shredded coconut

1 Tbsp superfood seed blend

¼ cup raspberries

Directions

1. Combine all smoothie bowl ingredients in a blender jar and blend until smooth and no chunks remain.

2. Pour into a bowl and add toppings.

> If the smoothie is too thick for your blender to handle, add more almond milk.

Berry Heart Beets

Emily Sunwell-Vidaurri of *Recipes to Nourish* (recipestonourish.com)

Richly pigmented with beautiful deep pink and purplish hues, this beet and berry smoothie is perfectly sweet with bright, earthy undertones. As an extra bonus, the beets help support the heart, digestion, and overall wellness.

Ingredients

Smoothie Bowl

1 medium beet

1 cup frozen strawberries

¼ cup frozen blueberries

1 frozen banana

½ cup plain whole milk yogurt

¼ cup milk or coconut milk

2 Tbsp raw honey

1 tsp vanilla extract

Toppings

1 fresh fig, halved

2 strawberries, sliced

5 blueberries, sliced

2 blackberries

1-inch chunk crystallized ginger, diced

½ tsp white chia seeds

Directions

1. Peel beet, cut into 1-inch cubes, and steam or boil until fork-tender. Spread cooked beets on parchment paper–lined baking sheet. Freeze for a minimum of 1 hour.

2. Combine beet with the rest of the smoothie bowl ingredients in a blender jar and blend until smooth and no chunks remain.

3. Pour into a bowl and add toppings.

Tip: Cook the beets and freeze at least a day prior to making the smoothie for a quicker smoothie bowl prep time.

A Bowl Full of Cherries

gf P df

This bowl is inspired by my favorite homemade popsicle recipe. Even though it includes the unusual ingredient zucchini, the flavor profile is actually cherry and lime. You can't taste the zucchini at all, but you do get its nutritional benefits!

Ingredients

Smoothie Bowl

1 small zucchini, roughly chopped
juice of 1 fresh lime (about 3 Tbsp)
1 Tbsp local honey
2 cups frozen dark sweet cherries

Toppings

1 cup fresh cherries

Directions

1. Combine zucchini, lime juice, and honey in a blender jar and blend until smooth and no chunks remain.

2. Add cherries and process until well blended.

3. Pour into a bowl and top with fresh cherries.

Look for the popsicle version of this recipe on my website, creativegreenliving.com.

Dark Berry

Dark fruits like açaí berries, blackberries, and raspberries are high in anthocyanins—a type of phytonutrient that studies show to be particularly effective in helping your body fight cancer. Oh, and did I mention they are delicious?!

Ingredients

Smoothie Bowl

- 1 small banana, peeled
- ½ cup frozen raspberries
- ½ cup frozen strawberries
- ½ cup frozen blackberries
- 1 (3.5-oz) pack frozen açaí
- ¾ cup coconut water

Toppings

- ⅓ cup dry coconut pieces
- ¼ cup fresh or frozen pomegranate arils
- ¼ cup raw cashews
- 3 fresh strawberries, halved

Directions

1. Combine all smoothie bowl ingredients in a blender jar and blend until smooth and no chunks remain.

2. Pour into a bowl and add toppings in rows on top of smoothie.

Getting the arils out of a fresh pomegranate doesn't have to be messy or frustrating. Visit my YouTube channel, *Creative Green Living*, for my secret trick for deseeding a pomegranate quickly.

Raspberry Lemonade Nice Cream

V gf df

Frozen lemonade is one of my favorite summertime treats. The trouble is: frozen lemonade only seems to be seasonally available at most restaurants. Not only that, but it's often full of high fructose corn syrup—a product usually made from GMO corn with a high concentration of processed sugar that isn't the least bit nourishing to your body. My raspberry lemonade recipe can be made year-round, and you can tailor the amount of agave to adjust how sweet or tart it is.

Ingredients

Smoothie Bowl

3 cups frozen raspberries

1 lemon, peeled

1 cup coconut water

2 Tbsp agave syrup

Toppings

fresh edible flowers like violas (pictured)

Directions

1. Combine all smoothie bowl ingredients in a high-powered blender or food processor and pulse until smooth and no chunks remain. Pause and scrape down sides as needed during the blending process.

2. Pour into a bowl and top with edible flowers.

For a probiotic boost, try this same recipe with 1 cup of lemon-flavored kombucha instead of coconut water.

Northwest Summer

A favorite summer pastime in the Pacific Northwest is fruit picking. While blackberries grow wild in just about every ditch or untended patch of land, blueberries and peaches are available at "U-pick" farms all over the area. This bowl combines all my favorite summertime fruits from the Northwest in one tasty bowl!

Ingredients

Smoothie Bowl

1 medium banana, peeled

½ cup frozen blackberries

1 cup frozen blueberries

½ cup frozen peaches

¾ cup coconut water

Toppings

¼ cup dry coconut pieces

⅓ cup raspberries

¼ cup raw cashews

4 fresh mint leaves

5 fresh violas (flowers)

Directions

1. Combine all smoothie bowl ingredients in a blender jar and blend until smooth and no chunks remain.

2. Pour into a bowl and add toppings.

For a more authentically Northwest experience, substitute crushed hazelnuts for the cashews in the toppings.

Razzle Dazzle Nice Cream (V) (P) (gf) (df)

This nice cream recipe is one of my family's favorites. Watermelon are not available here year-round, so during the summer, we'll buy extra to cut into chunks and freeze to use in recipes like this one.

Ingredients

Smoothie Bowl

2 cups frozen watermelon chunks

1 cup frozen raspberries

3 Tbsp açaí juice

Toppings

1 Tbsp shredded coconut

Directions

1. Combine all smoothie bowl ingredients in a food processor and pulse until smooth, stopping as needed to scrape down the sides.

2. Scoop into a bowl and top with coconut.

When preparing watermelon for freezing, be sure to spread the chunks out so they do not freeze together into one large brick.

Blissful Beet Berry

V P gf df

Anya Dzhangetov of *Prepare & Nourish* (prepareandnourish.com)

Sweetened with natural sugars from medjool dates, this smoothie has subtle hints of the earthy flavor from beets and boasts a high antioxidant level. A blend of seasonal berries gives it delicious dimension while the fat from the coconut milk aids in the nutrient assimilation of the beets and berries.

Ingredients

Smoothie Bowl

- 1 cup frozen strawberries or raspberries
- 1 cup frozen blackberries or blueberries
- 2 small cooked beets
- 1–3 medjool dates, pitted (optional for sweetness)
- 1 cup full-fat coconut milk

Toppings

- 1 tsp bee pollen
- 1 Tbsp roasted coconut chips
- ¼ cup fresh raspberries

Directions

1. Combine all smoothie bowl ingredients in a blender jar and blend until smooth and no chunks remain.

2. Pour into a bowl and add toppings.

Don't have dates on hand? Try using a frozen banana instead!

Peachberry Nice Cream (V) (P) gf df

This nice cream has a wonderful velvety texture just like a sorbet, but no ice cream maker is required to pull off this tasty treat! All you need is a fresh peach and some frozen strawberries for a healthy dessert perfect for any time of day.

Ingredients

Smoothie Bowl

½ fresh peach, sliced and pitted

2 cups frozen strawberries

Toppings

½ fresh peach, chopped

Directions

1. Combine all smoothie bowl ingredients in a food processor and pulse until smooth, stopping as needed to scrape down the sides. If needed, add additional fresh peach to facilitate processing.

2. Scoop into a bowl and top with chopped peach chunks.

This recipes works best with a perfectly ripe peach that isn't too firm.

Berry Party

Frederikke Wærens, on Instagram as @FrederikkeWaerens

This smoothie bowl has a fresh, sweet, and fruity flavor. It's perfect as breakfast or an afternoon snack, but you can also use it as a healthy dessert since the texture is similar to soft serve ice cream.

Ingredients

Smoothie Bowl

- 1 frozen banana
- 1 cup frozen raspberries
- ½ cup frozen strawberries
- ½ cup almond or other plant-based milk
- 1 tsp açaí powder
- 1 tsp vanilla powder or extract

Toppings

- ½ cup blueberries
- 3 strawberries, halved
- 5 raspberries
- 1 Tbsp coconut flakes
- 1 Tbsp chia seeds

Directions

1. Combine all smoothie bowl ingredients in a blender jar and blend until smooth and no chunks remain.

2. Pour into a bowl and add toppings.

Island Sunrise

Even though this smoothie bowl contains a full carrot, the dominant flavors are orange and pineapple. One of my friends who had been on the search for orange-flavored soft serve ice cream tried this and said that this recipe was everything she ever dreamed of in a creamsicle-flavored treat. If you have a hard time getting your kids (or spouse!) to eat vegetables, this might be a great way to sneak their veggies to them in a healthy "dessert."

Ingredients

Smoothie Bowl

1 carrot, top and tip removed, roughly chopped

1 cup fresh orange juice

1 Tbsp flaxseed

1¼ cups frozen pineapple chunks

1 cup frozen peach chunks

Toppings

2 strawberries, sliced

2 Tbsp dried coconut pieces

Directions

1. Combine all smoothie bowl ingredients in a blender jar and blend until smooth and no chunks remain.

2. Pour into a bowl and add toppings.

> If you don't have a high-powered blender, blend the carrot, orange juice, and flax-seeds first before adding the frozen fruit to make sure the carrot blends well and is not chunky.

Summer Sunset

Karissa Martindale of *Honeycomb Market* (honeycombmarket.com)

This smoothie is full of summer flavor. Sweet peaches are the star here, but when combined with the earthiness of green tea and the fresh bite of ginger, you have a winning combination. Get the taste of summer all year-round.

Ingredients

Smoothie Bowl

¾ cup brewed green tea, chilled

¼ cup raspberries

1½ cups frozen peaches

1 Tbsp hemp seed

2 tsp local honey

¼ tsp freshly grated ginger

Toppings

2 Tbsp blueberries

1 Tbsp toasted coconut

3–5 blackberries

3–5 raspberries

½ tsp hemp seeds

Directions

1. Combine all smoothie bowl ingredients in a blender jar and blend until smooth and no chunks remain.

2. Pour into a bowl and add toppings.

Freeze grated ginger in ½ teaspoon measures in a small ice cube tray. It will increase the shelf life of your ginger and give you the perfect amount for your next stir-fry or smoothie bowl. The cubes can go straight from the freezer into a blender or hot pan.

Tropical Twist Nice Cream (V) (P) (gf) (df)

Simple nice creams are my favorite on a hot day or any time I need a frozen treat! You'll be surprised how much you love this creamy concoction despite its low fat and sugar content!

Ingredients

Smoothie Bowl

1½ cups frozen strawberries

1½ cups frozen mango chunks

⅓ cup coconut or other plant-based milk

Toppings

1 Tbsp dried goji berries

Directions

1. Combine all smoothie bowl ingredients in a food processor and pulse until smooth, stopping as needed to scrape down the sides.

2. Scoop into a bowl and top with goji berries.

Peachy Keen

This smooth, creamy bowl is perfect on a hot summer day. It's also a great way to introduce yourself to kombucha. Some brands of kombucha can have a sour taste, but by using a lemonade flavor and blending it into a smoothie bowl, you get all of the probiotic benefits but none of the pucker.

Ingredients

Smoothie Bowl

1 cup frozen peaches
½ cup frozen mango chunks
½ cup frozen strawberries
1 cup lemonade-flavored kombucha
½ cup cold water

Toppings

½ cup fresh raspberries
small sprig of mint

Directions

1. Combine all smoothie bowl ingredients in a blender jar and blend until smooth and no chunks remain.

2. Pour into a bowl and add toppings

If you are already a kombucha lover, try making this recipe with 1½ cups kombucha instead of a mix of kombucha and cold water.

Sunshiney Day

This bowl is the perfect pick-me-up before tackling your long weekend projects list. The extra fiber boost from the carrots and cashews will keep you full while the antioxidants from the fruit and carrots keep you fired up. The fresh ginger gives a little bite to an otherwise sweet smoothie.

Ingredients

Smoothie Bowl

2 medium carrots, tops and tips
   removed, roughly chopped
1 cup orange juice
½-inch-piece fresh ginger, peeled
   and diced
1½ cups frozen peach chunks

Toppings

¼ cup fresh or frozen raspberries
2 Tbsp dried goji berries
2 Tbsp raw cashews
2 Tbsp fresh or frozen blueberries

Directions

1. Combine all smoothie bowl ingredients in a blender jar and blend until smooth and no chunks remain.

2. Pour into a bowl and add toppings.

To easily peel fresh ginger without cutting your fingers, try using the side of a spoon to scrape away the papery outer skin.

Orange Carrot Love

(V) (P) (gf) (df)

I love to pair citrus with carrots. Do you know how to make that combo even more amazing? Add ginger. Ginger, citrus, and carrots? Love indeed!

Ingredients

Smoothie Bowl

- 2 carrots, tops and tips removed, roughly chopped
- 1 mandarin, tangerine, or clementine, peeled
- 1-inch-piece fresh ginger, peeled
- 1 small banana, peeled
- ½ cup lemon-ginger-flavored kombucha
- 1 cup frozen peaches
- ¾ cup frozen pineapple

Toppings

- 1 tsp chia seeds
- ¼ cup raw cashew pieces

Directions

1. Combine all smoothie bowl ingredients except the peaches and pineapple in a blender jar and blend until smooth and no chunks remain.

2. Add the peaches and pineapple and process until well blended.

3. Pour smoothie into a bowl and add toppings, using cookie cutters as templates, if desired.

To make fun shapes with your toppings, gently place a cookie cutter on top of your smoothie bowl and spread the toppings in a thin layer inside the cutter before carefully removing. For this smoothie, I used one large heart cookie cutter and another small heart cookie cutter at the same time.

Sweet Potato Pie

Larisha Campbell of *We're Parents* (wereparentsblog.com)

Looking for a taste of Thanksgiving any time of year? Then this is the smoothie bowl that will feed your soul! Decadent, roasted sweet potatoes, creamy cashew milk, and more—blended with pumpkin pie spice—will send your mouth into overdrive.

Ingredients

Smoothie Bowl

- ½ sweet potato, cooked and cooled, skin removed
- 1 large carrot, top and tip removed, roughly chopped
- 1 frozen banana
- ½ cup plain Greek yogurt
- ½ cup cashew milk
- 1 Tbsp honey
- 1 Tbsp ground flaxseed
- 1 tsp pumpkin pie spice
- ½ tsp vanilla extract
- 10 ice cubes

Toppings

- 1 Tbsp chia seeds
- 2 Tbsp chopped unsalted cashews
- 2 Tbsp shredded coconut
- 1 Tbsp dried cranberries
- drizzle of plain Greek yogurt

Directions

1. Combine all smoothie bowl ingredients in a blender jar and blend until smooth and no chunks remain.

2. Pour into a bowl and add toppings.

Carrot Cake

While baking the perfect gluten-free cake is trickier than you might think, blending up the smoothie version of classic baked goods like pie, cake, and muffins is surprisingly easy. This smoothie bowl is also lower in sugar and more nutrient dense than a baked carrot cake—making it a perfect healthy swap for your favorite dessert.

Ingredients

Smoothie Bowl

2 medium carrots, tops and tips
    removed, roughly chopped
1 cup plain whole milk yogurt
½ cup rolled oats
2 tsp agave syrup
1 Tbsp flaxseed
¼ tsp pumpkin pie spice blend
1½ frozen bananas

Toppings

2 Tbsp shredded coconut
¼ cup mixed color raisins
2 Tbsp chopped nuts

Directions

1. Combine all smoothie bowl ingredients except frozen banana in a blender jar and blend until no chunks remain.

2. Add frozen banana and blend until smooth.

3. Pour into a bowl and add toppings.

Want more baked-goods-inspired smoothie bowls? You'll love these: Apple Pie (page 55), Cherry Cobbler (page 77), Sweet Potato Pie (page 126), and Blueberry Muffin (page 177).

Peachy Protein Powerhouse

Elizabeth Lindemann of *Bowl of Delicious* (bowlofdelicious.com)

gf

Sweet, refreshing, and packed with protein from whole milk yogurt and chia seeds, this smoothie bowl is the perfect way to recover from an intense workout on a hot summer's day (especially with the anti-inflammatory properties of strawberries), or to enjoy for breakfast to keep you full of energy all morning. A special trick is used to make the smoothie extra thick and creamy—soaking the chia seeds before blending!

Ingredients

Smoothie Bowl

- ¼ cup coconut water
- 2 Tbsp chia seeds
- ½ peach or nectarine, sliced and pitted
- 5 medium strawberries
- ½ cup plain whole milk yogurt
- 1 Tbsp honey (optional)

Toppings

- ½ peach or nectarine, sliced
- 1–2 strawberries, sliced
- 1 tsp chia seeds

Directions

1. Stir together coconut water and chia seeds. Allow to sit for at least 10 minutes.

2. Combine coconut/chia mix with remaining smoothie bowl ingredients in a blender jar and blend until smooth and no chunks remain.

3. Pour into a bowl and add toppings.

For a thicker smoothie bowl, use frozen fruit in place of fresh.

Pineapple Paradise

This sweet, pineapple-infused bowl will feel like a welcome to a tropical hideaway. The bright flavors are a great energizing start to your day.

Ingredients

Smoothie Bowl

- 1 banana, peeled
- ½ cup fresh orange juice
- ½ cup coconut or other plant-based milk
- 1½ cups frozen pineapple
- 1½ cups frozen peach chunks

Toppings

- 1 banana, peeled and sliced
- 3 strawberries, chopped
- 1 Tbsp granola

Directions

1. Combine all smoothie bowl ingredients in a blender jar and blend until smooth and no chunks remain.

2. Pour into a bowl and add toppings.

Smashing Pumpkin

gf

Melissa Potvin of *How to . . . This and That* (HowToThisAndThat.com)

This decadent bowl will remind you of Thanksgiving dessert at Aunt Mary's house. For the best results, use chilled pumpkin. If you don't have time to chill the pumpkin, try adding a frozen banana to the smoothie to chill it while blending.

Ingredients

Smoothie Bowl

½ cup puréed or canned pumpkin, chilled

⅔ cup plain Greek yogurt

⅓ cup almond milk

1 Tbsp maple syrup

½ tsp ground cinnamon

½ tsp ground nutmeg or allspice

Toppings

¼ cup raisins

¼ cup walnuts, chopped

2 Tbsp rolled oats

dash cinnamon

dash nutmeg

Directions

1. Combine all smoothie bowl ingredients in a blender jar and blend until smooth and no chunks remain.

2. Pour into a bowl and add toppings.

Sunny Days

In Oregon, it can get a little dreary during the winter. Truthfully, most of us like the cloudy, wet weather, but occasionally a craving for sunshine sets in. If sun isn't in the forecast, this is the next best thing! The bright colors and flavors will feel like a boost of sunshine on your cloudy day.

Ingredients

Smoothie Bowl

1 banana, peeled

½ cup orange juice

⅔ cup plain Greek yogurt

1½ cups frozen mango chunks

Toppings

1 strawberry, sliced

⅓ cup blackberries

1 sprig mint

Directions

1. Combine all smoothie bowl ingredients in a blender jar and blend until smooth and no chunks remain.

2. Pour into a bowl and add toppings.

Everything's Peachy

Michelle Marine of *Simplify, Live, Love* (simplifylivelove.com)

This is the perfect summer pick-me-up. Fresh peaches and berries make a delicious combination, and the addition of chia and hemp seeds add a superfood punch you will love.

Ingredients

Smoothie Bowl

2 cups frozen peach chunks

1 frozen banana

¼ cup plain whole milk yogurt

1 Tbsp local honey

Toppings

½ cup blackberries

¼ cup blueberries

2 Tbsp almond slivers

1 tsp chia seeds

1 tsp hemp seeds

Directions

1. Combine all smoothie bowl ingredients in a blender jar and blend until smooth and no chunks remain.

2. Pour into a bowl and add toppings.

Piña Colada Nice Cream

V P gf df

One of my favorite things I did last summer was learn how to crack open and use fresh coconuts and their meat. After some experimenting, this frozen concoction has become my favorite way to enjoy fresh coconut meat. As a fun bonus, the shell doubles as a bowl!

Ingredients

Smoothie Bowl

1 fresh coconut

3 cups frozen pineapple chunks

1 cup lime-flavored kombucha

Toppings

¼ cup fresh blackberries

Directions

1. Crack fresh coconut open, removing the white flesh from the shell of one half by inserting a spoon or a paring knife between the shell and the membrane surrounding the white flesh and prying away pieces (save the other half to be a serving bowl).

2. Put fresh coconut chunks into a food processor with the pineapple and kombucha. Pulse until well combined.

3. Scoop nice cream into the other half of the coconut. Top with blackberries and serve.

If this is your first time cracking open a coconut, see instructions on page 25 or visit my YouTube channel, Creative Green Living, to see a step-by-step tutorial for how to crack open a coconut and remove the meat.

Pineapple Kick

Jenni Ward of *The Gingered Whisk* (thegingeredwhisk.com)

Sweet, tropical pineapple and coconut combine beautifully into a smoothie bowl to get you in a vacation mood! It might taste like a dessert, but when you add the healthiest toppings around, this is a nutritional powerhouse. Speaking of powerhouses, this smoothie bowl gets a fun kick in the tastebuds from honey-roasted chipotle almonds! Just the right amount of sweet and spice!

Ingredients

Smoothie Bowl

2 cups frozen pineapple chunks

1 Tbsp lime juice

½ cup full-fat coconut milk

Toppings

¼ cup fresh pineapple, chopped

1 tsp chia seeds

1 Tbsp honey-roasted chipotle almonds

¼ cup granola

¼ cup shredded unsweetened coconut

2 Tbsp roasted, unsalted pumpkin seeds

generous drizzle of honey

Directions

1. Combine all smoothie bowl ingredients in a blender jar and blend until smooth and no chunks remain.

2. Pour into a bowl and add toppings.

Tangy Tropical Treat

V P gf df

Tracy Ariza of *Oh, the Things We'll Make!* (thethingswellmake.com)

Imagine yourself on a tropical beach while enjoying this smooth, tasty treat. It may not be the same as an island adventure, but it will brighten up your day, and it's healthier than a boozy piña colada.

Ingredients

Smoothie Bowl

- ½ mango, peeled, seed removed, and roughly chopped
- 1 cup frozen pineapple
- 1 peach, pitted and roughly chopped
- ½ cup full-fat coconut milk

Toppings

- 1 Tbsp flaxseed
- 1 Brazil nut
- 1 kiwi, peeled, sliced, and quartered
- 2 Tbsp raspberries
- ¼ cup blueberries
- 1 Tbsp hemp seeds

Directions

1. Prepare the flaxseed topping by blending together the flaxseed and Brazil nut in the blender until flaxseeds are completely ground. Remove from the blender and set aside.

2. Combine all smoothie bowl ingredients in a blender jar and blend until smooth and no chunks remain. Add more coconut milk as needed to aid in blending.

3. Pour into a bowl and add toppings.

I like to grind together about 1 cup of flaxseeds with a few Brazil nuts and store the mixture in the fridge to use as a topping for smoothie bowls or yogurt. I usually only make enough for a week or two at a time, as flaxseeds oxidize quickly once ground, which can cause their fatty acids to break down. The Brazil nuts add selenium and a nutty texture to the mixture.

Honeydew Nice Cream

gf P df

Do you have a fruit you like the flavor of but not the texture? For me, that's honeydew. Never one to give up easily, I decided to keep experimenting with ways to eat it and came up with this—which is perhaps the most amazing honeydew concoction ever! You get all the honeydew flavor, none of the waxy texture, and blueberries are the perfect companion.

Ingredients

Smoothie Bowl

½ fresh honeydew melon

1 Tbsp local honey

¼–½ cup full-fat coconut milk

Toppings

¼ cup blueberries

Directions

1. Scoop out and discard seeds from the melon. Cut away outer rind with a knife. Cut remaining flesh into chunks and freeze at least 4 hours.

2. Add frozen honeydew chunks, honey, and ¼ cup coconut milk to a food processor. Pulse until well combined. Add additional coconut milk as needed to facilitate smooth blending.

3. Scoop into a bowl or hollowed-out melon and top with blueberries.

For a fun serving idea, save the other half of the melon and scoop out the seeds to make a bowl.

Mermaid Magic Nice Cream

I'm a big fan of color in my food. The first nice cream I ever made was just frozen bananas and coconut milk—which meant is was a boring, off-white color. This nice cream builds on the original recipe, but adds a kiwi and spirulina for a boost of both color and flavor.

Ingredients

Smoothie Bowl

1½ kiwi, peeled

3 frozen bananas

2 Tbsp full-fat coconut milk

1 Tbsp honey

½ tsp spirulina powder

Toppings

¼ cup blackberries

Directions

1. Combine all smoothie bowl ingredients in a food processor and pulse until smooth, stopping as needed to scrape down the sides.

2. Scoop into a bowl and top with blackberries.

Spirulina powder is available in health food stores as well as online.

It Hass to be Good!

Melissa Potvin of *How to . . . This and That* (howtothisandthat.com)

My recipe highlights the beautiful Hass Avocado as the star. Throw in a few more ingredients and you have a satisfying, high-protein, super antioxidant treat that will keep you going all day.

Ingredients

Smoothie Bowl

½ Hass avocado, peeled and pitted

¼ cup kale, chopped

½ cup almond milk

⅔ cup plain Greek yogurt

1 Tbsp raw honey

Toppings

¼ cup blueberries

½ kiwi, peeled and sliced

2 Tbsp shelled sunflower seeds

2 Tbsp shredded coconut

Directions

1. Combine all smoothie bowl ingredients in a blender jar and blend until smooth and no chunks remain.

2. Pour into a bowl and add toppings.

Groovy & Green

Baby spinach is a great smoothie ingredient because it brings such a vibrant color with it. The flavor of spinach is mild, though, and easily masked by stronger flavors like pineapple and ginger.

Ingredients

Smoothie Bowl

1 large handful baby spinach

1 large banana, peeled (1 slice reserved for topping)

⅔ cup lemon-ginger flavored kombucha

1 cup frozen pineapple

1 cup frozen peaches

Toppings

1 banana slice

1½ tsp chia seeds

¼ cup blackberries

Directions

1. Combine all smoothie bowl ingredients in a blender jar and blend until smooth and no chunks remain.

2. Pour into a bowl and add toppings, using a large cookie cutter if desired to shape the chia seeds into a flower and place the reserved banana slice in the middle.

> To create shapes with your toppings, gently float a cookie cutter on top of your smoothie and sprinkle the topping inside the walls. Carefully lift the cookie cutter straight up when done.

Green-ya Colada

Piña colada is a favorite combination of mine. I decided to green up my favorite tropical treat with fresh baby spinach for added color and nutrition. The flavor of baby spinach is very mild, and so while you get all the nutritional benefits of raw spinach, it won't taste "grassy" like other smoothies containing greens can.

Ingredients

Smoothie Bowl

1 large handful fresh baby spinach

½ cup full-fat coconut milk

1 tsp agave syrup

1½ cups frozen pineapple

Toppings

1 strawberry and a piece of pineapple on a drink skewer

2 Tbsp shredded coconut

Directions

1. Combine all smoothie bowl ingredients except pineapple in a blender jar and blend until smooth and no pieces of spinach remain.

2. Add frozen pineapple to blender and blend until smooth.

3. Pour into a bowl and add toppings.

> For a fun serving dish alternative, cut a fresh pineapple in half and hollow out one side to use as a bowl.

Tropical Greens

Sam Ellis of *The Culinary Compass* (theculinarycompass.com)

This smoothie bowl is full of tropical flavors that will cool you off even on the hottest of summer days! You'll be full of energy and antioxidants with all the benefits that the matcha green tea powder brings.

Ingredients

Smoothie Bowl

¾ cup frozen mango

¼ banana, peeled

⅓ cup frozen pineapple

½ cup almond milk

½ cup spinach

½ tsp matcha powder

ice (as needed)

Toppings

2 Tbsp coconut flakes

⅓ cup mango, cubed

¼ cup pineapple, cubed

1 kiwi, peeled and cubed

Directions

1. Combine all smoothie bowl ingredients in a blender jar and blend until smooth and no chunks remain.

2. Pour into a bowl and add toppings.

Be sure to add the matcha powder to the blender after the almond milk to help keep it from clumping!

Pentatonic Kale

This recipe features both spinach and baby kale. If you aren't accustomed to the "green" flavor that accompanies green smoothies, use baby spinach in place of the kale—all you'll taste is the fruit!

Ingredients

Smoothie Bowl

½ cup baby kale, packed
½ cup baby spinach, packed
½ Tbsp chia seeds
1 Tbsp flaxseed
½ cup coconut water
1 kiwi, peeled
⅔ cup frozen pineapple
⅔ cup frozen peach chunks

Toppings

1 kiwi, peeled and sliced
1 Tbsp chia seeds
5 fresh raspberries
5 fresh blackberries
¼ cup dried coconut pieces
1 tsp sliced almonds

Directions

1. Combine kale, spinach, chia, flaxseed, coconut water, and kiwi in a blender jar and blend until smooth and no green bits remain.

2. Add frozen fruit and blend until smooth.

3. Pour into a bowl and add toppings.

Summer Paradise

Despite the bright green color, this smoothie has a very mild flavor. Baby spinach is useful that way—stunning color, boost of fiber and nutrients, no grassy taste! It's topped with my favorite fresh summer fruits, but if you're longing for a summer flavor mid-winter, frozen fruit makes a great topping, too.

Ingredients

Smoothie Bowl

1 large handful fresh baby spinach

¾ large banana, peeled

½ cup fresh orange juice

2 cups frozen peach chunks

Toppings

2 fresh strawberries, halved

2 Tbsp blueberries

1 Tbsp coconut flakes

¼ fresh peach, sliced

¼ banana, peeled and sliced

1 Tbsp dried goji berries

Directions

1. Combine spinach, banana, and orange juice in a blender jar and blend until smooth and no chunks remain.

2. Add frozen peaches and blend until smooth.

3. Pour into a bowl and add toppings.

Coconut flakes come in many different sizes, textures, and levels of sweetness. If you don't like the first type you try, keep experimenting until you find your favorite!

Green Monster

When I was in graduate school near Boston, my employer informed me that I was required to become a Red Sox fan if I wanted to work there. Even though I loved the Seattle Mariners, the Red Sox became my adopted team. One of the things I learned about during the countless Red Sox games I watched with the rest of the staff was The Green Monster—a large wall in Fenway Park—which is also the namesake of Wally, the Green Monster, the Red Sox's mascot. I like to think that after a hard day of dancing at the games, Wally would enjoy coming home to enjoy this nutritious beast to boost his energy and keep his colors bright!

Ingredients

Smoothie Bowl

- 3 large kale leaves, stalks removed
- 1 banana, peeled
- 1 small apple, peeled and cored
- ¾ cup coconut or other plant-based milk
- ¼ cup raw pumpkin seeds
- 1 Tbsp flaxseed
- 1-inch-piece fresh ginger, peeled
- 2 Tbsp local honey
- 1¼ cups frozen pineapple

Toppings

- 1 small banana, peeled and sliced
- 2 figs, cut into sections
- 2 Tbsp granola
- drizzle of honey

Directions

1. Combine all smoothie bowl ingredients except pineapple in a blender jar and blend until smooth and no chunks remain.

2. Add frozen pineapple and blend until smooth.

3. Pour into a bowl and add toppings.

Green Goodness

As you can imagine, smoothies and smoothie bowls are a staple in our home. Smoothie connoisseurs themselves, my kids often provide the inspiration for the smoothie bowls I make that day. This one was made at the request of my six-year-old son, who got to help decorate it with his favorite berries.

Ingredients

Smoothie Bowl

- 1 cup coconut or other plant-based milk
- 2 handfuls fresh baby spinach
- 1 banana, peeled
- ½ cup frozen pineapple
- ½ cup frozen peaches

Toppings

- ¼ cup fresh raspberries
- ½ cup fresh blackberries
- 1 Tbsp chia seeds

Directions

1. Combine coconut milk, spinach, and banana in a blender jar and blend until smooth and no green chunks remain.

2. Add frozen fruit and blend once more until all chunks are gone.

3. Pour into a bowl and add toppings.

Mighty Mint

Natasha Bull of *Salt & Lavender* (saltandlavender.com)

This green smoothie bowl is packed with good-for-you ingredients including spinach, avocado, and mint. The toppings add crunch, texture, and a bit of sweetness. Cacao nibs + mint = mint chocolate the healthy way!

Ingredients

Smoothie Bowl

½ avocado, peeled

1 frozen banana

1 cup spinach, lightly packed

1 tsp honey

1 tsp flaxseed

¼ cup mint, packed

½ cup unsweetened almond milk

4 ice cubes

Toppings

1 Tbsp dried goji berries

1 Tbsp shaved coconut

2 tsp cacao nibs

¼ cup granola

Directions

1. Combine all smoothie bowl ingredients in a blender jar and blend until smooth and no chunks remain.

2. Pour into a bowl and add toppings.

Instead of cacao nibs, you may also enjoy dark chocolate chips.

See You on the Color Side

This is an impressive-looking bowl to serve when you have guests or really want to wow your Instagram followers! You start with a green smoothie base and then magically make half purple by adding blueberries at the end!

Ingredients

Smoothie Bowl

1 large handful baby spinach

1 Tbsp flaxseed

1 cup coconut water, divided

1 banana, peeled

⅔ cup frozen pineapple

⅔ cup frozen mango

⅔ cup frozen blueberries

Toppings

1 Tbsp chia seeds

1 kiwi, peeled and sliced

1 Tbsp sliced almonds

¼ cup frozen blueberries

Directions

1. Add spinach, flaxseed, ½ cup coconut water, and banana to blender and blend on high until no chunks remain.

2. Add pineapple and mango, blending until no chunks remain.

3. Pour half of the smoothie into a bowl. Replace blender jar and add blueberries and ¼ cup coconut water. Blend on high, adding more coconut water as needed to ease blendability.

4. Pour purple smoothie over half of the bowl and add toppings.

Ocean Blue

Valerie Fidan, on Instagram as @ValerieFidan

Jump-start your day with a lip-smacking blend of superfood ingredients. This blue-green superfood smoothie bowl sensation is loaded with vitamins, ultra-powerful antioxidants from blue-green algae, plant-based protein, and fiber along with a tasty punch!

Ingredients

Smoothie Bowl

- 2 cups frozen Supergreens mix (baby spinach, baby kale, baby Swiss chard)
- 1¼ cups full-fat coconut milk
- ½ small avocado, peeled, cubed, and frozen
- ½ cup frozen blueberries
- 1 tsp blue-green algae/spirulina
- ¼ cup black sesame seeds
- 2 dates, pitted
- 1 tsp cinnamon

Toppings

- 1 Tbsp hemp seeds
- 1 Tbsp coconut shavings
- 6 roasted cashews
- 1 tsp black sesame seeds
- mint leaves, to taste
- ¼ cup blueberry and blackberry mix

Directions

1. Combine all smoothie bowl ingredients in a blender jar and blend until smooth and no chunks remain.

2. Pour into a bowl and add toppings.

To make smoothies easier to prepare the day-of, precube and freeze avocado halves and premeasure and freeze fresh supergreens blend in zip-top bags so they are ready to go when it's smoothie time!

Blueberry Muffin

When I first decided to stop eating gluten due to a medical condition, the one gluten-y food item I missed most was blueberry muffins. My personality is a "never ever ever give up" type, so even though I still couldn't eat wheat, I was set on figuring out a way to make a "blueberry muffin" possible. In this recipe, the oats and flax lend a muffin-y taste while also giving the smoothie wonderful body.

Ingredients

Smoothie Bowl

- ½ cup rolled oats
- ¾ cup plain whole milk yogurt
- splash vanilla extract
- 1 Tbsp flaxseed
- ¼ cup coconut or other plant-based milk
- 1 tsp agave syrup
- 1 cup frozen blueberries
- ½ frozen banana

Toppings

- 2 Tbsp granola
- ½ cup blueberries

Directions

1. Combine all smoothie bowl ingredients except blueberries and banana in a blender jar and blend until smooth and no chunks remain.

2. Add blueberries and bananas. Pulse and then blend until smooth.

3. Pour into a bowl and add toppings.

Rolled oats and granola are both ingredients that may be contaminated with gluten or wheat dust. Gluten-sensitive individuals should seek gluten-free versions of these ingredients.

Exotic Probiotic

Jyothi Rajesh of *Curry Trail* (currytrail.in)

The next best thing to ice cream is, of course, a smoothie bowl. For this creamy smoothie, I combined blueberries and yogurt to make a bowl rich in calcium and fiber. It's the perfect way to kick off your morning or to enjoy as a healthy snack after a workout.

Ingredients

Smoothie Bowl

1 cup frozen blueberries

¾ cup plain Greek yogurt

1 frozen banana

2 Tbsp maple syrup

1 tsp vanilla extract

Toppings

¼ cup blueberries

1 banana, sliced

4 strawberries, sliced

1 kiwi, peeled and sliced

1 tsp chia seeds

Directions

1. Combine all smoothie bowl ingredients in a blender jar and blend until smooth and no chunks remain.

2. Pour into a bowl and add toppings.

Matcha Berry Energy

(V) (P) (gf) (df)

Some may find the flavor of matcha powder to be overwhelming. The perfect solution to this problem is to mask the flavor with berries. This gives you an extra antioxidant boost plus the energy boosting benefits of matcha without the unusual flavor.

Ingredients

Smoothie Bowl

½ cup frozen blueberries

1 cup frozen strawberries

½ tsp matcha powder

¾ large banana, peeled

1 cup coconut or other plant based milk

Toppings

1 Tbsp chia seeds

¼ large banana, peeled and sliced

½ cup fresh blackberries

Directions

1. Combine all smoothie bowl ingredients in a blender jar and blend until smooth and no chunks remain.

2. Pour into a bowl and add toppings.

Morning Matchavation

If you're looking for a morning pick-me-up, skip the coffee and dive into this fresh bowl of goodness instead. Matcha provides an antioxidant boost that many claim boosts their energy as well as their memory and sense of calm. Try getting that from your average cup o' Joe!

Ingredients

Smoothie Bowl

- 1 large handful fresh baby spinach leaves
- ¾ large banana, peeled
- ½ cup coconut or other plant-based milk
- 1 tsp matcha green tea powder
- 1 kiwi, peeled
- 1 cup frozen peach chunks
- 1 cup frozen blueberries

Toppings

- ½ fresh peach, sliced
- 3 fresh strawberries, halved
- 6 fresh blackberries
- ¼ fresh banana, sliced
- ¼ cup granola
- 1 tsp chia seeds

Directions

1. Combine all smoothie bowl ingredients in a blender jar and blend until smooth and no chunks remain.

2. Pour into a bowl and add toppings.

If you have a hard time finding matcha green tea powder in your local store, there are several vendors who sell high-quality, organic matcha online.

Tropical Berry Breeze

gf P df

This bowl is made with grocery store staples that are available all year—which makes it ideal for whipping up a tropical treat when the winter doldrums set in. Blend up this bowl any time to create a culinary getaway.

Ingredients

Smoothie Bowl

1 cup frozen blueberries

1 cup frozen cherries

1 Tbsp flaxseed

1 cup açaí juice

1 Tbsp local honey

Toppings

1 kiwi, peeled and sliced

2 Tbsp shaved coconut pieces

Directions

1. Combine all smoothie bowl ingredients in a blender jar and blend until smooth and no chunks remain.

2. Fill a clear glass bowl ⅓ of the way with the prepared smoothie. Line up kiwi slices, pressed against the glass on the sides, and then fill bowl with remaining smoothie. Top with coconut.

Sacre-Blue!

The delightful combination of açaí, orange, and blueberries in this antioxidant-rich bowl will have you proclaiming your love for all-things blue from the rooftops. Although, for you introverted types, a simple "yum!" will suffice.

Ingredients

Smoothie Bowl

- 2 (3.5-oz) packs frozen açaí
- 1 cup orange juice
- 1 small banana, peeled
- 1 cup frozen blueberries

Toppings

- 2 fresh strawberries, halved
- 1 tsp chia seeds
- 1 Tbsp plain puffed rice or quinoa cereal
- 2 Tbsp dried coconut chunks

Directions

1. Combine all smoothie bowl ingredients in a blender jar and blend until smooth and no chunks remain.

2. Pour into a bowl and add toppings.

3. Serve with additional fresh fruit on the side if desired.

Unsweetened puffed rice and quinoa cereals are a fun way to add extra crunch and texture to your smoothie bowl.

Açaí Supercharge

High in nutrients, especially antioxidants, açaí berries are a wonderful way to fuel your cells to power through your day. Some may find the taste to be unusual, but by combining açaí with the sweetness of banana and a little bit of honey, you get a tasty treat that is perfectly balanced.

Ingredients

Smoothie Bowl

- 1 (3.5-oz) pack frozen açaí
- 1 banana, peeled
- 1 kiwi, peeled
- 1 Tbsp local honey
- 1 cup frozen blueberries
- ½ cup coconut or other plant-based milk

Toppings

- 2 Tbsp shredded coconut
- ½ kiwi, peeled and sliced
- edible flowers

Directions

1. Combine all smoothie bowl ingredients in a blender jar and blend until smooth and no chunks remain.

2. Pour into a bowl and add toppings.

Flowers are a fun way to garnish smoothie bowls. Not all flowers are edible, though. A good rule of thumb is: if you aren't sure, don't eat it!

Fig Love

Figs are still considered a novelty in many markets. At a recent gathering of girlfriends, only about 10 percent of them had ever eaten a fresh fig. Figs' soft skins are beautifully blendable, and fig wedges make a great smoothie bowl garnish. If fresh figs are not in season, try looking for them in the frozen fruit section of your grocery or specialty-food store.

Ingredients

Smoothie Bowl

1 banana, peeled

3 fresh figs, stems removed

¾ cup coconut water

1 Tbsp local honey

½ cup plain Greek yogurt

1 Tbsp chia seeds

1 cup frozen blueberries

1 cup frozen black raspberries

Toppings

1 small banana, peeled and sliced

1 fig, stem removed and cut into wedges

1 Tbsp granola

Directions

1. Combine all smoothie bowl ingredients in a blender jar and blend until smooth and no chunks remain.

2. Pour into a bowl and add toppings.

If black raspberries are not available in your area, use blackberries or red raspberries in their place.

Dark Forest

When fresh cherries are in season, I love using them to make smoothie bowls! For this recipe, I use frozen cherries to give the smoothie bowl body and fresh cherries to garnish the top. Using a lavender-flavored kombucha not only contributes beneficial probiotics, but also a subtle floral flavor that combines well with the cherries.

Ingredients

Smoothie Bowl

½ cup frozen dark cherries

1 cup frozen blueberries

½ cup lavender-flavored kombucha

½ cup water

1 Tbsp chia seeds

Toppings

⅓ cup diced apple

⅓ cup fresh cherries, halved with pits removed

1 small sprig of mint

2–4 edible flowers

Directions

1. Combine all smoothie bowl ingredients in a blender jar and blend until smooth and no chunks remain.

2. Pour into a bowl and add toppings.

Edible flowers that make great smoothie bowl garnishes include violas, pansies, borage, roses, and calendula. Just be sure they are grown without pesticides.

For a stronger floral flavor, use 1 cup lavender-kombucha instead of a mix of kombucha and water.

Blackberry Delight

Every summer, families in Oregon and Washington look forward to the wild blackberry bushes making abundant, free blackberries that are tastier than any you can buy in the store. The summer I was writing recipes for this book, my oldest son was enamored with blackberries. He asked me to come up with something that combined peach, blackberry, and pineapple. When he asked if he could name my recipe Blackberry Delight, how could I say no?

Ingredients

Smoothie Bowl

1 cup frozen peach chunks

1 cup frozen blackberries

1 Tbsp chia seeds

1½ cups coconut or other plant-based milk

Toppings

1 fresh pineapple spear, sliced

2 Tbsp granola

½ banana, peeled and sliced

Directions

1. Combine all smoothie bowl ingredients in a blender jar and blend until smooth and no chunks remain.

2. Pour into a bowl and add toppings.

> If you are avoiding gluten, be sure to look for a granola labeled "gluten free," as some granola recipes contain wheat-based ingredients.

Black and Blue Nice Cream

Sometimes the best recipes are the simplest. This nice cream has just three ingredients, but tastes every bit as indulgent as your favorite premium ice cream!

Ingredients

Smoothie Bowl

1 cup frozen blackberries
1 cup frozen blueberries
1 medium banana, peeled

Toppings

¼ cup fresh blueberries

Directions

1. Combine all smoothie bowl ingredients in a food processor and pulse until smooth, scraping down the sides of the bowl as needed.

2. Scoop into a bowl and top with blueberries.

Surf Rider

Kiwi and berry are a timeless combination. A tart, ripe kiwi balanced by sweet berries is enough to make any mouth sing! The addition of raw cashews to this classic combo gives the bowl just the right amount of crunch.

Ingredients

Smoothie Bowl

2 kiwis, peeled

1¾ cups frozen blueberries

¾ cup brewed green tea, chilled

Toppings

1 kiwi, peeled and sliced

¼ cup blueberries

2 Tbsp raw cashews

Directions

1. Combine all smoothie bowl ingredients in a blender jar and blend until smooth and no chunks remain.

2. Pour into a bowl and add toppings.

Purple Cow Nice Cream

gf

When I attended graduate school in Massachusetts, I was introduced to an ice cream flavor that soon became my favorite: Purple Cow. Purple Cow ice cream is a black raspberry ice cream with both dark and white chocolate chips mixed in. It's delightful. This recipe is an ode to my favorite New England ice cream flavor with a healthy twist and a fraction of the sugar.

Ingredients

Smoothie Bowl

1 frozen banana
1½ cups frozen black raspberries
¼ cup full-fat coconut milk
¼ cup plain whole milk yogurt
1 tsp agave syrup

Toppings

1 tsp dark chocolate chips
1 tsp white chocolate chips

Directions

1. Combine all smoothie bowl ingredients in a food processor and pulse until smooth, pausing to scrape down the sides as needed.

2. Scoop into a bowl and top with chocolate chips.

For extra protein, substitute Greek yogurt for the whole milk yogurt.

Açaí Bliss

Jasmin White of *Healthy Twenties* (healthytwenties.co.uk)

Superfoods meets super seeds in this powered-up breakfast bowl. Packed with vitamins and antioxidants, this açaí smoothie makes the perfect nutritious breakfast.

Ingredients

Smoothie Bowl

2 frozen bananas
½ cup frozen blueberries
¼ cup fresh orange juice
2 Tbsp açaí powder

Toppings

½ banana, sliced and cut into shapes
¼ cup blueberries
2 Tbsp raspberries
1 Tbsp mixed seeds (I used a blend of chia, hemp, and flaxseed)

Directions

1. Combine all smoothie bowl ingredients in a blender jar and blend until smooth and no chunks remain.

2. Pour into a bowl and add toppings.

Not a fan of seeds? Try topping your açaí bowl with granola instead!

To make fun flower shapes, use mini cookie cutters to cut out flowers from the banana slices.

Berries 'n Booch

Pacific Northwest summers are often full of wild berries and cold tea. Of course, in Portland, it wouldn't be unusual to find that our "cold tea" has been fermented into kombucha. While many find kombucha to be an acquired taste, using it in a smoothie helps cover up the tangy flavor if you're not a fan. Experiment using different kombucha flavors in this smoothie to find the flavor combo you love the most!

Ingredients

Smoothie Bowl

1 cup frozen strawberries

1 cup frozen blackberries

1½ cups kombucha

Toppings

¼ cup fresh cherries

2 Tbsp apple, chopped

1 Tbsp raw cashews

¼ cup blueberries

Directions

1. Combine all smoothie bowl ingredients in a blender jar and blend until smooth and no chunks remain.

2. Pour into a bowl and add toppings.

> If you don't have kombucha on hand, try using brewed black or green tea instead.

Purple Dragon Nice Cream

gf

I love color. Anytime I can make something in a pretty, saturated color, I do it. For this recipe, I used pink-fleshed pitaya (as opposed to white) to get this pretty purple when it combined with the blueberries and black raspberries. Enjoy!

Ingredients

Smoothie Bowl

1½ cups frozen blueberries

1 cup frozen black raspberries

1 cup frozen dragon fruit (pitaya) chunks

⅓ cup blueberry kefir

1 Tbsp agave syrup

Toppings

1 kiwi, peeled and sliced

Directions

1. Combine all smoothie bowl ingredients in a food processor and pulse until smooth, stopping as needed to scrape down the sides.

2. Scoop into a bowl and top with kiwi slices.

Kefir is a fermented dairy product similar to a drinkable yogurt. Look for kefir in the dairy case at your local grocery store. Can't find kefir? Use whole milk yogurt instead.

Greenberry

No matter how good the smoothie tastes, sometimes the color green is really off-putting to people. Whether it was a bad experience with Brussels sprouts as a child or it just happens to be someone's least favorite color, it's not easy being a green smoothie bowl. This bowls comes with all of the benefits of the greens—but none of the "scary" color.

Ingredients

Smoothie Bowl

- 1 small handful baby spinach leaves
- 1 small handful baby kale leaves
- 1 small banana, peeled
- 1 tsp agave syrup
- ¾ cup lemon flavored kombucha
- 1¼ cups frozen blueberries
- 1¼ cups frozen blackberries

Toppings

- ⅓ cup fresh or frozen blueberries
- ¼ cup granola

Directions

1. Combine all smoothie bowl ingredients except frozen berries in a blender jar and blend until smooth and no chunks remain.

2. Add frozen berries to blender jar and blend until smooth.

3. Pour into a bowl and add toppings.

If you are avoiding gluten, be sure to select a granola labeled as "gluten free."

Join Me on a
Smoothie Bowl Journey

My goal with this book was to inspire you to branch out and experiment. Whether you're new to smoothie bowls or new to superfoods, I hope I will inspire you to try at least one new thing. If you are feeling adventurous, I hope you will try many new things!

As you are branching out and experimenting, share your experiments with others! You never know who you might encourage with your healthier choices. I would love to see pictures of your smoothie bowl creations on Instagram (be sure to use #BeautifulSmoothieBowls). You can also Snap, Facebook, Tweet, or share photos as part of your review of this book through your favorite online bookstore. I also invite you to join me online. You can find me on Instagram as @CreativeGreenLiving. I also have a food-specific Instagram account as @CreativeGreenKitchen, where I share my latest smoothie bowl creations and other healthy recipes. I also moderate a wonderful, supportive community on Facebook called the Creative Green Living Community Group. Creative Green Living is in reference to my website, www.CreativeGreenLiving.com, and the group is full of people interested in healthy choices they can make in their lives that are still beautiful and delicious—just like these smoothie bowls!

Recipe Contributor Credits

I'm so grateful to each of these contributors for being a part of bringing *Beautiful Smoothie Bowls* to you. Each of these recipe developers has a website or an Instagram (or both!) where you can connect with them, get more fabulous recipes, and see more beautiful food photos. As you try the recipes and find your favorites, be sure to connect with the authors and follow them on social media to get more of the great stuff you love!

Note: If the recipe does not have an author listed, the recipe was developed by me, Carissa Bonham. Visit me online at www.CreativeGreenLiving.com or on Instagram as @CreativeGreenLiving and @CreativeGreenKitchen.

Tracy Ariza

Tracy is an American expat who lives in Spain and blogs at *Oh, the Things We'll Make!* (www.thethingswellmake.com) and in Spanish at www.CosasCaseras.com. She loves figuring out how to make anything from papadums to homemade soaps from scratch and shows you how easy it can be to make your own natural products and foods. Healthy food should never be bland and boring, so she shares fun, simple, gluten-free recipes that the whole family will love. Join her on her adventures in Spain on Instagram as @thethingswellmake.

Natasha Bull

Natasha, founder of *Salt & Lavender* (www.saltandlavender.com), is a Canadian food blogger who has a serious love affair with her barbecue. She lives in Edmonton, Alberta, but her heart is in warmer places. Natasha prefers her recipes to be easy to prepare so that she has time for the important things in life, like drinking prosecco with her husband while watching NASCAR, hockey, and the Denver Broncos.

Larisha Campbell

Larisha and her husband, Andrew, run *We're Parents*, a unique mom-and-dad natural parenting blog focusing on their "semicrunchyish" life, recipes kids love, and family travels. They live in New Jersey with their two beautiful daughters. You can find them at www.wereparentsblog.com and at @wereparents on all social media sites.

Anya Dzhangetov

Anya is the founder and author behind *Prepare & Nourish* (www.prepareandnourish.com), a place where she shares her passion for traditional, healthy, and delicious foods. She enjoys re-creating her traditional Slavic recipes with nourishing ingredients while sharing good food with amazing friends around her handcrafted farmhouse table in Northern California. She can be found on Instagram as @prepareandnourish.

Sam Ellis

Sam is the blogger behind *The Culinary Compass*, where she loves to try new dishes and ingredients from around the world. She hopes to bring experiences of new cultures to her readers without having to leave their homes. Follow along on her blog at theculinarycompass.com or on Instagram as @TheCulinaryCompass to try something new!

Valerie Fidan

Valerie is a self-proclaimed foodie, inspired by the coastal lifestyle. When she's not health-hacking recipes for her blog LetsRegale.com, cooking (and blending) up a storm, or snapping millions of food photos on Instagram as @ValerieFidan, she works as a social media strategist in the craft beer industry in Portland, Oregon.

Caroline Ginolfi

Caroline is a plant-based recipe developer and health coach certified in plant-based nutrition. She works with individuals suffering from chronic conditions and teaches them how to manage, reverse, and prevent illness through a whole foods, plant-based lifestyle. She lives outside of Philadelphia, Pensylvania, and is mom to a rescue pup. Find her on Instagram as @plantbasedblonde or visit her webpage www.plantbasedblonde.com.

Sara Jansson

Sara lives in the archipelago just outside of Stockholm and works full time (with something completely different than food). She is the mother of two adorable little children and she spends much of her spare time preparing and shooting healthy food and treats. When not working or in the kitchen you'll find her out running in the forest, swimming in the open waters, or doing yoga on the jetty. See more of her work on Instagram as @swimyogarun.

Elizabeth Lindemann

Elizabeth runs the food blog, *Bowl of Delicious*. Her recipes and posts are about "Real Food for Busy People"—they're made from whole ingredients and are freezer friendly, make-ahead, slow-cooker friendly, or quick and easy. Follow her at www.bowlofdelicious. com and as @bowlofdelicious on Instagram, Twitter, and Facebook!

Michelle Marine

Michelle blogs at SimplifyLiveLove.com and is a crunchy mama of four living on five acres in Eastern Iowa. She values real food and enjoys feeding her family smoothies using ingredients she grows herself. A self-proclaimed chicken fanatic, Michelle also enjoys reading, traveling, cooking, and CrossFit. Find her on Instagram as @SimplifyLiveLove.

Karissa Martindale

Karissa is the food and photography enthusiast behind the blog, *Honeycomb Market* (honeycombmarket.com). When she's not whipping up something delicious, you can find her scouring antique markets for one-of-a-kind pieces. Tag along on all her grand adventures in and out of the kitchen on Instagram as @honeycombmarket.

Landen McBride

Landen is a food and minimalist living blogger. There are few places she would rather be than in her kitchen. She hails from Austin, Texas, and bakes constantly for her husband and little boy. You can find her recipes at www.measureandwhisk.com and gorgeous photos of her daily cooking adventures on Instagram as @measureandwhisk.

Elizabeth Menlove and Sarah Romero

Elizabeth and her daughter, Sarah Romero, are a mother-daughter cooking combo who love creating healthy recipes made from fresh and natural ingredients! Their food blog, *Kiwi and Carrot* (www.kiwiandcarrot.com) has hundreds of simple but delicious recipes including complete menus to make your meal planning easy.

Suchi Modi

Suchi is a food blogger at *Elegant Meraki* (www.elegantmeraki.com). She is a self-taught baker and photographer. She loves sweets, so she turns to fresh smoothies and juice for a sweet treat that helps her stay fit. Visit her website for delicious baking recipes with a unique flair.

Melissa Potvin

Melissa is a self-taught home chef who fuels her passion for cooking by writing original recipes and sharing them with readers through her blogs HowToThisAndThat.com and Clean-EatingRecipes.com. When she isn't working, she loves spending time with her family traveling and enjoying nature.

Jyothi Rajesh

Jyothi writes about easy and creative recipes on her blog, *Curry Trail*. Her food is mostly influenced from her Indian roots. She lives in Bangalore, India, with her husband and two beautiful kids. After working several years in IT as a software engineer, she quit her job to start her own company offering robotics training for children. Food has always been her passion so she eventually forayed into food blogging, food styling, and food photography. Visit her website at currytrail.in or on Instagram as @currytrail.

Maja Redlin

Maja is a German food blogger who loves to inspire people with her vegan and vegetarian recipes that don't require expensive ingredients. She likes to keep it simple, healthy, and tasty. You can find more recipes on her blog: www.majardln.com, on Instagram as @majardln and on YouTube as Maja Redlin.

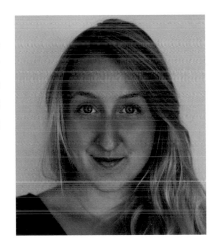

Sammi Ricke

Sammi, from the blog, *Grounded & Surrounded*, likes to keep things simple, delicious, and nutritious in her kitchen. She enjoys the challenge of finding unique ways to incorporate "just one more whole food" into every meal while leaving enough room for life's essentials: chocolate and peanut butter. If you are looking for "healthified" versions of your family's favorite recipes, be sure to visit Sammi's blog at www.groundedandsurrounded.com.

Abbey Sharp, RD

Abbey is a Media Registered Dietitian (RD), national spokesperson, TV and radio personality, YouTuber, food writer and blogger, recipe developer, and the founder of Abbey's Kitchen (www.abbeyskitchen.com). Abbey is a regular on national shows like The Marilyn Denis Show (CTV) and the Shopping Channel and is a monthly contributor to publications like *Best Health* magazine and *Fitness* magazine. Abbey has worked as a celebrity brand ambassador and spokesperson for dozens of popular food brands and runs a highly successful YouTube channel (youtube.com/abbeysharpabbeyskitchen) and a food blog called *Abbey's Kitchen*. Follow her for healthy cooking tips and nutrition myth busters on social media @AbbeysKitchen!

Katherine Mae Stanley

Katherine blogs at *Nourishing Simplicity* (nourishingsimplicity .org). She is a small-space homesteader living in the Central Valley of California. She thinks that mason jars with wildflowers, a cup of tea, and dark chocolate should be a part of every day.

Emily Sunwell-Vidaurri

Emily, founder and author of *Recipes to Nourish*, is a kombucha- and chocolate-loving, holistic-minded mommy of two little loves, and wife to one handsome cowboy. She's a real foodie, passionate about home cooking, lover of seasonal food, and she daydreams about being an urban homesteader. Emily blogs at *Recipes to Nourish* (www.recipestonourish.com), a gluten-free blog focusing on Real Food + Holistic Health. Connect with her on Instagram as @recipestonourish.

Frederikke Wærens

Frederikke is from Copenhagen, Denmark. She runs her own company for social media and photography and frequently collaborates with brands on design-related projects. Her interests include delicious food, interior and exterior architecture, and food photography. You can follow her on Instagram as @frederikkewaerens— where she has more than 200,000 followers, and on her YouTube channel: Frederikke Wærens.

Jenni Ward

Jenni blogs at *The Gingered Whisk* (www.thegingered whisk.com) and believes that food should be easy to prepare, delicious to eat, and nutritious enough to thoroughly enjoy. She lives in Iowa and loves teaching her children to explore and love the world of food.

Sara Welch

Sara is a food photographer, recipe developer, and food writer. She runs the blog *Dinner at the Zoo* (dinneratthezoo.com), where she shares family-friendly dinner ideas with some sweet treats on the side. Her photography has been featured in dozens of online publications, from Buzzfeed to *Redbook Magazine*. When she's not in the kitchen, Sara is busy chasing after her three young children.

Jasmin White

Jasmin has recently ventured into the world of blogging after the success of her Instagram page @healthytwenties. Explore more of her delicious plant-based recipes and beautiful photography over at www.healthytwenties.co.uk.

Resources

In putting together this book, my goal was to keep things very approachable by using easy-to-find ingredients and equipment. You should be able to find most smoothie bowl equipment at your local department store and ingredients at your local grocery store. For an up-to-date list of places to purchase my favorite equipment and ingredients online, visit: www.creativegreenliving.com/p/smoothie-bowl-resources.html.

For further reading

- To learn more about brewing your own kombucha at home to use in smoothie bowls or drinking on its own, see: *The Big Book of Kombucha* by Hannah Crum (2016, Storey).
- To learn about creating your own beneficial fermented beverages, including kombucha and kefir, see: *Delicious Probiotic Drinks* by Julia Mueller (2014, Skyhorse).
- For more delicious smoothie recipes using healthy superfood ingredients, see: *The Healthy Smoothie Bible* by Farnoosh Brock (2014, Skyhorse).

Acknowledgments

I want to thank my husband, Joe, and sons, Kaypha and Asher, for eating *so many* smoothie bowls during the summer of 2016 while I did recipe development and testing for this book. A big thank-you as well to my friends and family who let me feed them smoothie bowls during that same summer—especially my dad, who is far from a "smoothie bowls kind of guy."

I'm fortunate to be surrounded by an amazing tribe of bloggers and Instagrammers who cheered for me and supported me in this endeavor—from my "Gold" bloggers, to Liz Dean and the "Instagram Posse" to my fellow "Eco-Warriors," "Greenies," and "Shifters"—you know who you are, and I thank you for being a meaningful support team during the process of making this book a reality!

Part of this marvelous food blogger support team is Karissa Martindale from *Honeycomb Market*. Near the end of the process of getting this book together, I needed help getting about a dozen recipes re-photographed. Karissa stepped up to help me and did a fabulous job. Truly, this book would not have been done on time if it were not for Karissa's talent and assistance. I've held a theory for more than a decade that Carissas (of all spellings) are each super talented, creative people, and Karissa's great work more than supported this hypothesis! Her photos are marked with a photographer credit and I hope you will enjoy them as much as I do.

Finally, I want to acknowledge and thank my editor at Skyhorse Publishing, Nicole Frail, who made my dreams come true the day she emailed me asking me what I wanted to write a book about. I'm so glad she took the chance on me as a first-time author of something other than web content and eBooks. She stuck with me through the process of writing my first traditionally published book and put a great team in place to make this book a reality (thank you, team!).

For the dedicated readers of *Creative Green Living*, most especially members of the "Creative Green Living Community Group" on Facebook, thank you for your encouraging words and requests that I put out more cookbooks following my first eBook, *Infused*. I hope you I didn't let you down!

Index

Conversion Charts

(These conversions are rounded for convenience)

Ingredient	Cups/Tablespoons/ Teaspoons	Ounces	Grams/Milliliters
Agave, honey, or maple syrup	1 tablespoon	.75 ounce	20 grams
Fruit, dried	1 cup	4 ounces	120 grams
Fruits or veggies, chopped	1 cup	5 to 7 ounces	145 to 200 grams
Fruits or veggies, puréed	1 cup	8.5 ounces	245 grams
Liquids: cream, milk, water, or juice	1 cup	8 fluid ounces	240 milliliters
Oats	1 cup	5.5 ounces	150 grams
Spices: cinnamon, cloves, ginger, or nutmeg (ground)	1 teaspoon	0.2 ounce	5 milliliters
Vanilla extract	1 teaspoon	0.2 ounce	4 grams

Liquids

8 fluid ounces = 1 cup = ½ pint

16 fluid ounces = 2 cups = 1 pint

32 fluid ounces = 4 cups = 1 quart

128 fluid ounces = 16 cups = 1 gallon

LATIN
LOVER

Título original: *Latin Lover. Detti latini per tutte le occasioni*

© 2018, Edizioni EL
via J. Ressel 5, 34018 San Dorligo della Valle (Trieste), Italia

© 2018, de esta edición, Combel Editorial, SA
Casp, 79 – 08013 Barcelona
Tel. 902 107 007

combeleditorial.com

Primera edición: septiembre de 2018
ISBN: 978-84-9101-427-0
Depósito legal: B-17450-2018
Impreso en Índice, SL
Fluvià, 81-87 - 08019 Barcelona

LATIN

FRASES·LATINAS·PARA·TODAS·LAS·OCASIONES

LOVER

MINO MILANI

Ilustraciones de
SARA NOT

Adaptación de
CELIA FILIPETTO

COMBEL

1 AD KALENDAS GRAECAS

NUNCA

En la antigua Roma las *calendas* indicaban el primer día de cada mes. De esa palabra deriva el sustantivo *calendario*, que es el sistema que divide el tiempo en períodos. Al parecer, el gran emperador romano Augusto utilizaba esta frase. Cuando uno de sus ministros le informaba, por ejemplo, de que una ciudad, un gobierno o un determinado ciudadano tenían una deuda con el imperio, exclamaba malhumorado: «¡Vaya, esos nos pagarán en las calendas griegas!». O sea, nunca, porque en Grecia las calendas no existían.

2 AD MAIORA

HACIA COSAS MÁS GRANDES

Estas palabras de felicitación son muy bonitas. Pero diría que están destinadas a quien ya ha hecho cosas buenas o incluso grandes; me parece que quieren expresar: «Has estado muy bien, lo has hecho bien. Por lo tanto, eres capaz de hacerlo mejor. ¡Hazlo!». Si me las dijeran a mí, aunque lo veo difícil, creo que contestaría: «Gracias, haré lo que pueda, pero me gustaría ser yo quien decida qué hacer, es decir, aquello que nos resulta posible a todos en los estudios, en el trabajo, en la familia y en la amistad: cosas más grandes, pero no imposibles».

ARGH

3 ALEA IACTA EST

LA SUERTE ESTÁ ECHADA

Los dados, esas piezas cúbicas que antes eran de marfil o madera, y en cada cara llevan los números del 1 al 6, se usaban y se siguen usando, en juegos de azar en los que nos encomendamos a la suerte y no a la habilidad. Echado el dado, la suerte también estaba echada. Desde luego no se trató de un juego sino de una empresa muy peligrosa la que se propuso Julio César al cruzar el río Rubicón para marchar con su ejército contra Roma e iniciar la guerra civil, un hecho gravísimo. El dado está echado, la decisión está tomada. Vencer o morir sin posibilidad de retroceder.

ARBITER ELEGANTIARUM

ÁRBITRO DE LA ELEGANCIA

Así, a primera vista, nos da por pensar en alguien que va por ahí vestido con ropa de buen gusto y hechura perfecta que, si sumamos los precios desde los zapatos a la corbata, puede llegar a costar un riñón. Lo digo bien claro: a mí no me interesa. Pero parece ser que los romanos (que relacionaron la frase con Cayo Petronio, amigo del emperador Nerón) no se referían a sus ropas sino a sus gustos, a su forma perfecta de moverse, de hablar y de pensar. En ese caso, me vestiría de fiesta y me acercaría a esa persona para estrecharle la mano.

5 AUDACES FORTUNA IUVAT

LA FORTUNA AYUDA A LOS AUDACES

No lo dudemos ni un segundo, si los audaces enfilan el camino adecuado, la fortuna posa la mano en sus cabezas y los protege. La historia de Italia ofrece un ejemplo un tanto asombroso. El 6 de mayo de 1860, un millar de italianos, poco o mal armados, guiados por el general Giuseppe Garibaldi, partieron rumbo al Sur a bordo de dos barcos para derrotar al Reino de las Dos Sicilias y unificar Italia. Pensadlo: mil contra un reino, una locura. Pero la suerte estuvo de su parte y vencieron.

6 CARPE DIEM

DISFRUTA DEL MOMENTO

Un momento dura muy poco, lo sabemos. Como un parpadeo, ahora está y ya ha pasado. Puede anunciarse o no, eres tú quien lo siente, nadie más, solo tú decides. Quizá traiga consigo una buena ocasión, la suerte o incluso la felicidad. Si lo sientes así, en cuanto tengas la sensación de que ha llegado el momento que esperabas o soñabas, no lo dejes escapar. Aprovéchalo, porque no está claro que vuelva a presentarse. Pero ¿y si después me llevo un chasco? ¿Y si no es como espero que sea? ¡Ni te lo plantees! ¡Aprovéchalo! ¡Ay! ¿Lo ves? Ya ha pasado.

CASUS BELLI

MOTIVO DE GUERRA

Por desgracia, en el mundo hay muchas guerras. Son muchos los motivos que nos llevan a pelearnos y, si no existen, nos los inventamos. La historia está llena de ejemplos de que para comenzar una guerra se buscaba una excusa y si no la había, se creaba: un falso incidente, unos bandidos contratados para atacar una frontera, lo que fuese con tal de crear un *casus belli*. Se trata de un método lamentablemente vigente en nuestros días y que contradice la Carta de las Naciones Unidas que determina que las diferencias deben resolverse por medios pacíficos.

8 CAVE CANEM

¡CUIDADO CON EL PERRO!

En la entrada de una casa con jardín, casi todos nosotros hemos visto alguna vez esas placas en las que se advierte de la presencia de un perro. ¿A que sí? Llevan esta inscripción: «Cuidado con el perro», o bien «Cuidado, el perro muerde», o incluso «Llamen al timbre, perro guardián». Es una suerte que avisen. Esas advertencias las heredamos directamente de los romanos, tal como se puede ver, por ejemplo, en las excavaciones de Pompeya. Tanto es así que en alguna se lee el aviso en latín: *Cave canem*. Nuestros queridos amigos de cuatro patas llevan siglos vigilando nuestras casas.

9 COGITO ERGO SUM

PIENSO, LUEGO EXISTO

En efecto. Y para demostrarlo, recordemos que hubo alguien que observó: «¡No es así! Sino lo contrario: Existo, luego pienso». Pues no. Por desgracia hay muchísimas personas que existen (es decir que existen en el mundo), pero no piensan ni a tiros; todo lo contrario, dejan que sean otros quienes piensen por ellas, y dan la razón a quien dice lo que les gusta, o a quien grita más, y dejan que sean esos otros quienes se tomen el trabajo (es un decir) de pensar y decidir: «Esto está bien, esto está mal». Son muchos los que lo hacen así, ¿qué se creerán que es la vida? ¿Dejar que pasen los años sin creer, elegir ni pensar nada? Qué poquita cosa, ¿no?

10 CONDITIO SINE QUA NON

CONDICIÓN INDISPENSABLE

Hay frases y frases: algunas, a fin de cuentas, tienen buena intención (como *cave canem*), pero otras son severas e incluso podemos decir que resultan antipáticas. Como esta. Poner condiciones es algo legítimo y útil, porque de esta manera logramos entendernos sobre algún tema y se evitan complicaciones pero, en general, las condiciones *sine qua non* suelen ser un tanto molestas. No se discute. Todo o nada. O las tomas o las dejas. Como las lentejas...

CUI PRODEST?

¿A QUIÉN BENEFICIA?

¿Os gusta la novela negra, es decir, las historias de policías? A mí, sí. En general, te atrapan, están llenas de misterios y sorpresas. Y casi todas terminan bien, con el descubrimiento del culpable y la victoria del investigador que lo primero que hace es pensar así: se ha cometido un delito, y los delitos no se cometen porque sí, sino por un motivo; debo averiguar qué impulsó a quien cometió el crimen a llegar hasta ese punto, si descubro el móvil, encuentro al asesino. Los romanos ya habían pensado en ello. ¿A que eran unos genios?

12 CUM GRANO SALIS

CON UNA PIZCA DE SAL

Hay dos maneras de entender la palabra *sal*: una se relaciona con la cocina, la otra con la gracia. Si a una comida le falta sal, decimos que está sosa. Cuando a una persona le sobra chispa y buen humor, decimos que es muy salada. Con mucha gracia o con poca sal, esta frase suele utilizarse para dar a entender que no hay que tomarse las cosas al pie de la letra sino con un poquito de criterio.

DE GUSTIBUS NON EST DISPUTANDUM

SOBRE GUSTOS NO HAY QUE DISPUTAR

Para que algo sea de gusto basta que guste. De manera que el gusto siempre acierta, siempre tiene razón. Si algo (lo que sea, un hecho, una persona, una acción) no te gusta, te incomoda, te da asco, de nada sirve que traten de convencerte de lo contrario. Cuando era niño detestaba la coliflor y ahora me encanta, de lo que puede deducirse que con el tiempo los gustos cambian y que por ello no merece la pena ponerlos en tela de juicio.

14 DEUS EX MACHINA

UNA AYUDA DIVINA

No vayáis a imaginar que Dios baja en una nave espacial. No es nada por el estilo. En Roma y en la antigua Grecia, cuando en el teatro una obra dramática alcanzaba un punto complicado y los espectadores se quedaban turulatos y les entraban escalofríos, desde lo alto llegaba un dios o una diosa que lo arreglaba todo. El actor que interpretaba a la divinidad descendía sobre la escena montado en un complicado artilugio, la *machina*, y era recibido por los aplausos del público.

15 DO UT DES

DOY PARA QUE DES

Unas palabras muy acertadas, porque en el fondo todos hacemos las cosas para recibir una compensación. Por ejemplo, quien trabaja ofrece su empeño, su tiempo y su diligencia a cambio de un sueldo. Hay quien ve en la frase un punto de egoísmo: solo doy para conseguir algo a cambio, por nada más. Triste. Quien hace un regalo debería conformarse con una sonrisa y un «gracias».

16 DULCIS IN FUNDO

LO DULCE ESTÁ EN EL FONDO

A menudo aunque no siempre, esta frase podría referirse a que las mejores cosas llegan al final. Probablemente, quien se la inventó pensaba en eso. Sin embargo, los golosos son más simples y sostienen que el postre (las tartas, los pastelitos, las cremas, etcétera) se sirven al final de la comida, por eso no conviene atiborrarse con los platos que vienen antes.

17 DURA LEX SED LEX

LA LEY ES DURA, PERO ES LA LEY

El pueblo romano, tal vez mucho más que cualquier otro, cambió la historia del mundo. Para hacerlo no se limitó a conquistarlo y a construir caminos, puertos, ciudades y puentes, sino que dotó a su gran imperio de leyes sabias y obligaron a aplicarlas. Leyes duras, como lo eran todas en aquella época, y, sobre todo, inexorables: el que metía la pata, fuera quien fuese, era castigado. El cónsul Bruto supo que sus dos hijos habían conspirado y, siendo tan poderoso, los podría haber salvado: pero la ley era la ley y los mandó ejecutar.

18 ERRARE HUMANUM EST, PERSEVERARE DIABOLICUM

ERRAR ES HUMANO, PERSEVERAR EN EL ERROR, DIABÓLICO

Al leer la frase a toda prisa nos da por pensar: ¿por qué cuando te equivocas dos o tres veces, enseguida sacan a relucir al diablo? ¿No es un poquito exagerado? Si ese fuera el sentido de la expresión, sí, sería exagerado. Pero no lo es. Perseverar no quiere decir *repetir*, sino *insistir con firmeza*. De manera que no hay dudas: si uno se equivoca y sigue equivocándose aun sabiéndolo, mal asunto. Se tratará entonces de una estupidez o de algo deshonesto, en cuyo caso, es posible que el diablo haya hecho de las suyas.

19 HOMO HOMINI LUPUS

EL HOMBRE ES UN LOBO PARA EL HOMBRE

Dicen que el lobo es enemigo del hombre y de los rebaños de ovejas pero, en realidad, ataca cuando tiene hambre, nunca cuando tiene la barriga llena. Eso lo diferencia de algunos hombres que, a la menor ocasión, se aprovechan de la debilidad de sus semejantes. De estos hombres sí que podríamos decir que son lobos para los otros hombres. Pero por suerte, no todos son así.

20 IN MEDIO STAT VIRTUS

LA VIRTUD ESTÁ EN EL MEDIO

Francamente, no tengo muy claro qué es la virtud. En pocas palabras, ¿será tal vez la fuerza del corazón y la mente que nos impulsa a vivir respetando el bien y, por lo tanto, es una suma de pensamiento y acción? Si es así, no debería estar en el medio, sino de un solo lado. Nada de un poquito de bien y un poquito de mal, un poquito de corrección y un poquito de incorrección. ¿Qué sentido tiene entonces esta frase que suena tan bien? ¡Bah! Quizá lo que pretende es aconsejarnos que tampoco exageremos en eso de ser perfectos.

21 IN VINO VERITAS

EN EL VINO ESTÁ LA VERDAD

Lo que son las cosas. Para encontrar la verdad, es decir, aquello que se ajusta a la realidad, hubo filósofos que meditaron largo y tendido, sabios que escribieron libros, hombres que entraron en guerra. Para los romanos, en cambio, la verdad estaba en una copa de vino. Mejor dicho, en lo que le pasa a un tímido cuando, por ejemplo, después de beberse unas cuantas copas encuentra el valor de abrir su corazón y decir en voz alta lo que piensa, ama y cree. En una palabra, su verdad (pero ojo con beber demasiado...).

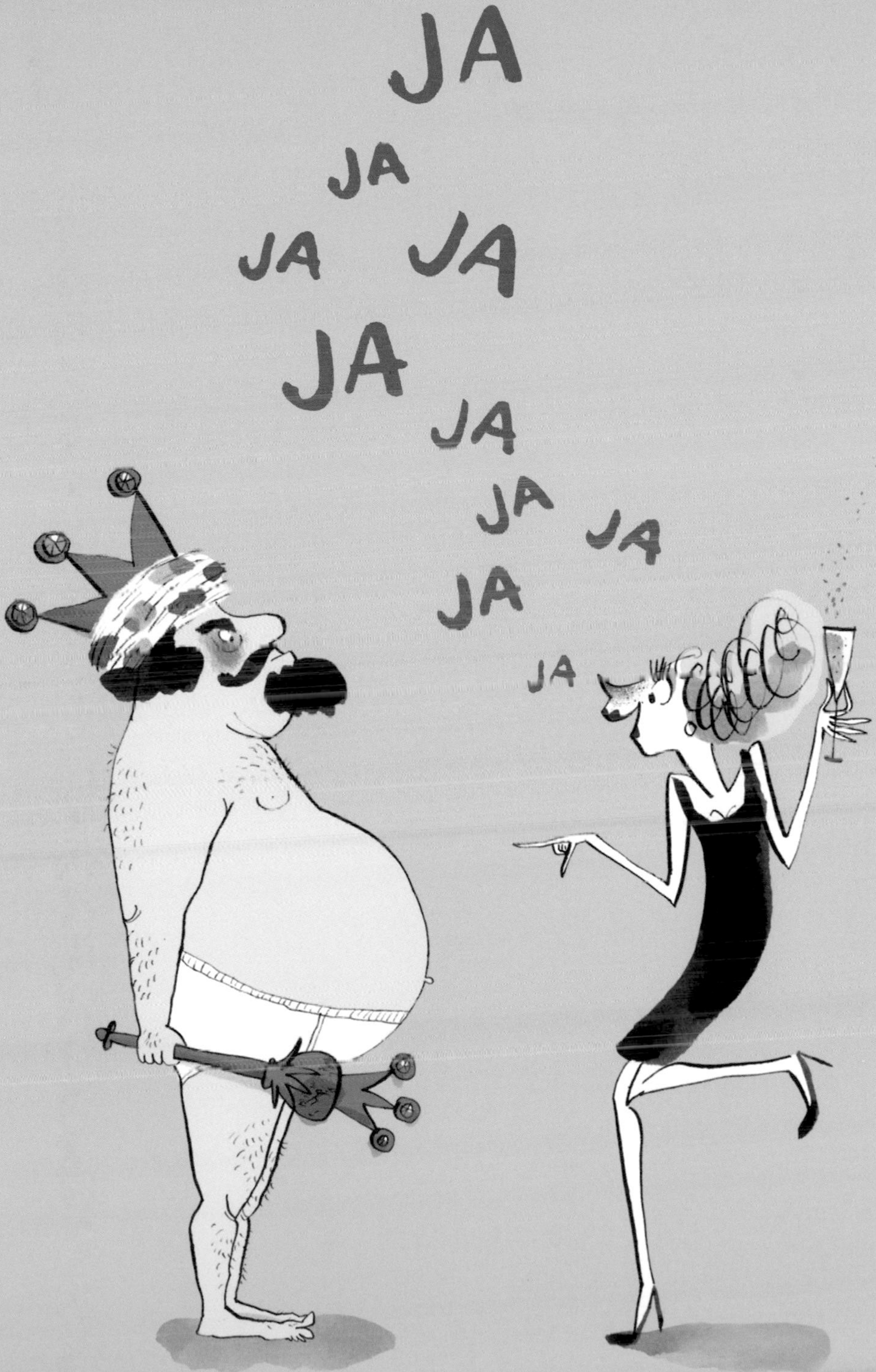
JA
JA
JA JA
JA
JA
JA
JA
JA
JA

22

IPSE DIXIT

ÉL LO DIJO

Si lo dijo él, no se hable más, todo está resuelto y se acabó la discusión. Vaya chiste. ¿Os gusta que os hablen así? ¿A que no? ¿Y qué se habrá creído ese «él» para que después de haber dicho una cosa ya no se pudiera añadir nada más? Se trataba nada menos que del gran filósofo Aristóteles. Pero ojo, era un hombre demasiado sabio e inteligente para soltar semejante frase. Probablemente la dichosa expresión la utilizaban sus discípulos para taparle la boca a los demás y ahorrarse el tener que discutir.

23

LUPUS IN FABULA

EL LOBO EN LA FÁBULA

La verdad es que no se entiende bien la expresión. Pongamos un ejemplo. Si estamos comentando que hace mucho que no vemos a Perico, y en ese preciso momento lo vemos aparecer, solemos exclamar: «¡Ahí viene!». En esa misma situación, los romanos decían: «*¡Lupus in fabula!*». Es decir, «Fíjate, hablábamos del lobo y ahí aparece». Desde luego no tenían la menor intención de insinuar que su amigo fuera peligroso. Era más bien una forma humorística de indicar que el lobo llegaba con solo mencionarlo. En español decimos: «Hablando del rey de Roma, por la puerta asoma».

24 MALA TEMPORA CURRUNT

CORREN MALOS TIEMPOS

Se trata de una frase que últimamente oímos con cierta frecuencia. No estamos seguros de que los romanos la utilizaran, porque a ellos las cosas les fueron de perlas durante unos cuantos siglos, y si después les fueron mal es porque la Historia no se detiene y tiene sus altibajos. Corren malos tiempos cuando un pueblo se siente cansado, nadie obedece a nadie. No hay trabajo y por eso aumenta la pobreza. Pero basta de quejas, por favor. Si la Historia tiene sus altibajos, significa que hoy estás abajo y mañana, quizá, estés arriba. Como las oscuras golondrinas, los buenos tiempos también volverán.

25 MELIUS ABUNDARE QUAM DEFICERE

ES MEJOR TENER DE SOBRA QUE CARECER

Vaya ocurrencia. ¿Quién no sabe que es preferible que te sobren salud, bondad, amigos, cultura a que te falten? Todo el mundo lo sabe. Se pueden discutir muchas de estas expresiones e incluso no estar de acuerdo con ellas, pero esta es indiscutible, porque se refiere a cosas útiles, buenas y favorables y no a las contrarias.

26 MEMENTO MORI

RECUERDA QUE HAS DE MORIR

Palabras muy duras donde las haya. Dicen una gran verdad y valen para todos, pero proyectan una sombra sobre la vida que vivimos. ¿Qué hacemos? ¿Las borramos, las olvidamos y mandamos a paseo a quien las escribió? Pues no. Lo mejor es pensar que forman parte de la vida, que debemos vivir por completo y a fondo, con sus alegrías y sus penas. Pero te doy un consejo: cuando decidas meditar sobre su profundo sentido, elige un momento tranquilo, de paz con los demás y, en especial, contigo mismo.

27 MENS SANA IN CORPORE SANO

MENTE SANA EN CUERPO SANO

Pues bien, esto no depende solo de nosotros, de nuestros propósitos. Sin duda, la salud y la inteligencia son los bienes más preciados, pero no siempre se nos ofrecen y no siempre a todos nosotros. De los muchos misterios de la vida y la naturaleza este es, sin duda, uno de los más incomprensibles. Sin embargo, también es cierto que podemos conseguir mucho si nos proponemos no llevar una vida desordenada y ociosa, optar por lo más fácil. ¿O sea que libros y gimnasia, estudio y algo de deporte? Sí, quizá sea la única receta.

28 NEMO PROPHETA IN PATRIA

NADIE ES PROFETA EN SU TIERRA

¿Sabéis quién pronunció estas palabras? Jesús. La frase quiere decir que a quien tenga ideas nuevas, grandes planes jamás pensados, le costará mucho llevarlos a cabo en su propia ciudad, allí donde todo el mundo lo conoce. Es así. Siempre saldrá alguien que diga: «¿Cómo es posible? Era mi compañero del colegio, uno del montón». O bien: «¿Ese se las da de genio? ¡Si aprobaba todo por los pelos!». Lo mejor es irse a otro lugar. No por miedo. Para quien siente que tiene cosas importantes que hacer, su tierra es el mundo entero.

NOMEN OMEN

EL NOMBRE ES UN PRESAGIO

Con este adagio latino se quería significar que nuestros nombres y apellidos nos caracterizan, llevan consigo una especie de advertencia o previsión del cómo será nuestro carácter y de cómo seremos en la vida. Aunque yo conocí a una chica cargada de soberbia que se llamaba Modesta, imaginaos, y mi querido amigo Hércules es delgado y come como un pajarito. De modo que de acuerdo, *nomen, omen,* como decían los latinos sirve, pero también al revés.

30 ORA ET LABORA

REZA Y TRABAJA

Se trata de la divisa o de la orden que San Benito dio a sus monjes y ha adquirido justa fama. De hecho, invita a dos actividades bien distintas pero que, unidas, son un verdadero programa de vida. El trabajo, realizado con las manos o la mente, permite mantener a raya el ocio y ganarse la vida; y la oración, el pensamiento dirigido a Dios, a sí mismos, al futuro, distingue al hombre de todos los demás seres vivos.

31 PECUNIA NON OLET

EL DINERO NO HUELE

Yo diría que no, haced la prueba. No huele a nada. En las lavanderías de la antigua Roma recogían en toneles la orina humana, la sometían a un tratamiento que permitía utilizarla como quitamanchas. Como el emperador Vespasiano andaba escaso de dinero, decidió cobrar un impuesto por esa orina. Su hijo Tito le reprochó: «Padre, ¿cómo puedes gravar toneles de material maloliente?». El emperador contestó tan tranquilo: «Pero el dinero que recaudamos no huele». Hay quien dice que estas palabras podrían justificar cualquier manera de hacer dinero. A saber.

32 QUALIS PATER, TALIS FILIUS

CUAL EL PADRE, TAL EL HIJO

No debemos pensar en un parecido físico. No siempre padre e hijo, hermano o hermana, madre e hija se parecen. La expresión se refiere más bien al carácter. Del mismo modo que heredamos el color de los ojos y el pelo, o la estatura, también podemos heredar la forma de ser, hacer y hablar, e incluso las ideas de los padres. De tal palo, tal astilla, decimos en castellano, pero caben aún muchas diferencias. Por ejemplo, mi padre detesta el brócoli y a mí me encanta.

33 REPETITA IUVANT

REPETIR LAS COSAS FAVORECE

«Niños, repetid conmigo...». Han pasado muchos años desde que fui a la escuela, pero todavía resuenan en mis oídos estas palabras de mi maestra. Ella decía: «Con diez cañones por banda», y nosotros repetíamos: «Con diez cañones por banda»... «Viento en popa, a toda vela», y nosotros recitábamos: «Viento en popa, a toda vela». Y así hasta el final de aquel precioso poema. De no haberlo repetido, tal vez no se me habría grabado en la memoria y en el corazón.

34 RISUS ABUNDAT IN ORE STULTORUM

LA RISA ABUNDA EN LA BOCA DE LOS NECIOS

En general, dicen que la gente que se ríe mucho piensa poco. Pero en mi curso había una chica a la que llamábamos «Sehamuertomitía», así todo junto, porque se reía todo el rato y sin motivo, y estábamos seguros de que, si se le hubiese muerto una tía, no sé si se hubiese reído, pero seguramente habría sonreído. Desde luego no era ninguna tonta. Además, ahora es una bisabuela cariñosa que ríe y sonríe a sus bisnietos. Es su forma de ser. A mí me parece que es mejor que los que no se ríen nunca y van por la vida muy serios y con cara de pocos amigos.

35 SEMEL IN ANNO LICET INSANIRE

ES LÍCITO UNA VEZ AL AÑO HACER UNA LOCURA

Me apresuro a aclarar que la frase se refiere a ir de juerga, a divertirse con los amigos, como en carnaval, por ejemplo. Aunque diría que una vez al año me parece demasiado poco. No se puede (mejor dicho, no se debe) estudiar, trabajar y estar serio el año entero. De vez en cuando se puede parar un poco, ¿no? Una vez me dio por parar, hice novillos y me fui por ahí a divertirme en grande. ¡Pero ay! No era carnaval y me castigaron.

TEMPUS FUGIT

EL TIEMPO HUYE

Ah, sí, huye, el tiempo, huye. Aunque no siempre. A veces se detiene. Hacen falta unos cuantos años para darse cuenta. Alguno me dirá: anda ya, una hora dura sesenta minutos. Sí, claro, en el reloj es así, pero el tiempo no depende únicamente del reloj, también depende de nosotros, de lo que hacemos, de lo que debemos hacer, de lo que sentimos. Si no hacemos nada y nos aburrimos, es como si el tiempo se detuviera y no pasara nunca. Si debemos hacer algo a toda prisa y vamos con retraso, entonces el tiempo se nos va en un pispás y es entonces cuando decimos: «¿Cómo es posible? ¿Ya las seis? ¡Si hace un minuto eran las cinco!».

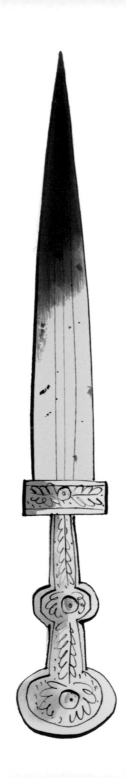

37 TU QUOQUE, BRUTE, FILI MI?

¿TAMBIÉN TÚ, BRUTO, HIJO MÍO?

Como sabemos, Roma era una república y lo fue durante siglos. En el año 44 a.C. un grupo de fanáticos republicanos sospechó que el invicto Julio César, poderoso y amado por el pueblo, quería convertirse en rey y decidieron asesinarlo. El 15 de marzo (los famosos idus de marzo), fue sorprendido a traición y apuñalado a muerte. Entre los asesinos estaba el joven Marco Junio Bruto, al que el César tenía gran aprecio. Al verlo levantar el puñal le dijo estas sentidas palabras y no intentó defenderse.

38 UBI MAIOR MINOR CESSAT

DONDE HAY SUPERIOR, CESA INFERIOR

Esta frase no suele gustar, no por eso es menos acertada. Si en deporte eres mejor que yo, si me ganas corriendo, saltando o nadando, yo tengo que aceptarlo. Es decir, si me ganas, lo aceptaré con un suspiro. Pero puede haber algo en lo que seguro no me ganarás: las ganas de mejorar.

39 VENI VIDI VICI

LLEGUÉ, VI Y VENCÍ

En el lejano año 63 a.C. los romanos conquistaron el Ponto, el escarpado territorio sobre el Mar Negro. Tiempo después, el joven príncipe Farnaces, que quería reinar en esas tierras, los echó. Acudió de inmediato el general romano Julio César, analizó la situación, se enfrentó a Farnaces y lo derrotó en la batalla de Zela. «*Veni, vidi, vici*» fueron las palabras con las que César comunicó al Senado su victoria. Había llevado a cabo lo que hoy se denomina una *Blitzkrieg*, una guerra relámpago.

VERBA VOLANT, SCRIPTA MANENT

LAS PALABRAS VUELAN, LOS ESCRITOS PERMANECEN

Dicen que las palabras se las lleva el viento, pero eso no significa que podamos decir la primera barbaridad que se nos pase por la cabeza y quedarnos tan anchos pensando que no nos pasará nada. Por eso, mucho cuidado con las palabras, porque pueden hacer daño. Ahora bien, si son palabras que queremos recordar, o si se refieren a un asunto importante, lo mejor es que las pongamos por escrito.

ET CETERA

Y LAS DEMÁS COSAS

41 **AD HOC**
A PROPÓSITO

42 **AD HONOREM**
A TÍTULO DE HONOR

43 **AD INTERIM**
PROVISIONALMENTE

44 **AD LIBITUM**
A CAPRICHO

45 **AD PERSONAM**
PARA UNA PERSONA DETERMINADA

46 **ALIBI**
COARTADA

47 **ALTER EGO**
OTRO YO

48 **ANTE LITTERAM**
ANTES DE TIEMPO

49 **AUT AUT**
O ESTO O LO OTRO, HAY QUE
ELEGIR ENTRE DOS COSAS
IRRECONCILIABLES

50 **BIS**
REPETICIÓN

51 **BREVI MANU**
ENTREGADO PERSONALMENTE

52 **CURRICULUM**
RELACIÓN DE TUS
CONOCIMIENTOS Y EXPERIENCIAS

53 **DE VISU**
DE VISTA, POR HABERLO VISTO

54 **DEO GRATIAS**
GRACIAS A DIOS

55 **ERRATA CORRIGE**
LISTA DE ERRORES LOCALIZADOS
TRAS LA IMPRESIÓN DE UN LIBRO

56 **FAC SIMILE**
COPIA EXACTA

57 **FAC TOTUM**
PERSONA QUE SE OCUPA DE TODO

58 **FORMA MENTIS**
ESTRUCTURA MENTAL

59 **GRATIS**
SIN PAGAR

60 **GROSSO MODO**
DE FORMA APROXIMADA

61 IN CALCE
A PIE DE PÁGINA

62 IN EXTREMIS
EN EL ÚLTIMO MOMENTO

63 IN FIERI
EN TRANCE DE HACERSE

64 IN FLAGRANTI
PILLAR A ALGUIEN CON LAS
MANOS EN LA MASA

65 IN ILLO TEMPORE
EN AQUEL TIEMPO

66 IN LOCO
EN EL LUGAR

67 IN MEDIAS RES
EN MEDIO DE LAS COSAS

68 IN NUCE
EN FORMA EXTRACTADA

69 IN PRIMIS
EN PRIMER LUGAR

70 IN TOTO
COMPLETAMENTE

71 IN VITRO
EN LA PROBETA

72 INTER NOS
DICHO ENTRE NOSOTROS,
EN CONFIANZA

73 LAPSUS
RESBALÓN, ERROR

74 MARE MAGNUM
CONFUSIÓN, BARULLO

75 MEMORANDUM
LO QUE HAY QUE RECORDAR,
NOTA

76 MINUS HABENS
DISCAPACITADO

77 MODUS OPERANDI
MODO DE OBRAR

78 NON PLUS ULTRA
NO HAY TIERRA MÁS ALLÁ

79 OBTORTO COLLO
A REGAÑADIENTES

80 OPERA OMNIA
OBRAS COMPLETAS

81 PAR CONDICIO
EL MISMO TRATO

82 PATER FAMILIAS
CABEZA DE FAMILIA

83 PLURALE MAIESTATIS
PLURAL MAYESTÁTICO

84 POLLICE VERSO
CON EL PULGAR VUELTO
HACIA EL SUELO EN SEÑAL
DE DESAPROBACIÓN

85 POST SCRIPTUM
DESPUÉS DE LO ESCRITO,
POSDATA

ÍNDICE